Kayaking

Outdoor Adventures

Library of Congress Cataloging-in-Publication Data

Kayaking / editors, Pamela S. Dillon, Jeremy Oyen.
    p. cm. -- (Outdoor adventures)
  ISBN-13: 978-0-7360-6716-4 (soft cover)
  ISBN-10: 0-7360-6716-7 (soft cover)
  1.   Kayaking--Handbooks, manuals, etc.   I. Dillon, Pamela II. Oyen, Jeremy, 1970-
  GV783.K39 2009
  797.122'4--dc22

                            2008032111

ISBN-10: 0-7360-6716-7
ISBN-13: 978-0-7360-6716-4

This publication and DVD are written, published, and produced to provide accurate and authoritative information relevant to the subject matter presented. It is published and sold with the understanding that the author and publisher are not engaged in rendering legal, medical, or other professional services by reason of their authorship or publication of this work. If medical or other expert assistance is required, the services of a competent professional person should be sought.

The Web addresses cited in this text were current as of August 2008, unless otherwise noted.

Acquisitions Editor: Gayle Kassing, PhD; **Developmental Editor:** Melissa Feld; **Assistant Editors:** Rachel Brito and Anne Rumery; **Copyeditor:** Patricia L. MacDonald; **Proofreader:** Kathy Bennett; **Permissions Manager:** Martha Gullo; **Graphic Designer:** Nancy Rasmus; **Graphic Artist:** Patrick Sandberg; **Cover Designer:** Keith Blomberg; **Photographer (cover):** U.S. Coast Guard; **Photographer (interior):** Mark Anderman/The Wild Studio unless otherwise noted. See pages 231-232 for a complete listing. **Photo Asset Manager:** Laura Fitch; **Photo Office Assistant:** Jason Allen; **Art Manager:** Kelly Hendren; **Associate Art Manager:** Alan L. Wilborn; **Illustrators:** Argosy and Alan L. Wilborn; **Printer:** United Graphics

Printed in the United States of America   10   9   8   7   6   5   4   3   2   1

Human Kinetics
Web site: www.HumanKinetics.com

United States: Human Kinetics
P.O. Box 5076
Champaign, IL 61825-5076
800-747-4457
e-mail: humank@hkusa.com

Canada: Human Kinetics
475 Devonshire Road Unit 100
Windsor, ON N8Y 2L5
800-465-7301 (in Canada only)
e-mail: info@hkcanada.com

Europe: Human Kinetics
107 Bradford Road, Stanningley
Leeds LS28 6AT, United Kingdom
+44 (0) 113 255 5665
e-mail: hk@hkeurope.com

Australia: Human Kinetics
57A Price Avenue
Lower Mitcham, South Australia 5062
08 8372 0999
e-mail: info@hkaustralia.com

New Zealand: Human Kinetics
Division of Sports Distributors NZ Ltd.
P.O. Box 300 226 Albany
North Shore City
Auckland
0064 9 448 1207
e-mail: info@humankinetics.co.nz

Kayaking

Outdoor Adventures

American Canoe Association

Editors

Pamela S. Dillon

Jeremy Oyen

HUMAN KINETICS

Contents

Preface

Welcome to *Kayaking*. In an effort to provide a resource to all outdoor enthusiasts, this introduction to kayaking has been developed for all current and future paddlers, including recreational paddlers who want to be safe on local ponds or streams and adventure seekers looking to move on to whitewater or coastal waters. The book also serves as a text for introductory kayaking courses taught at the university level.

This book was written in cooperation with the American Canoe Association (ACA). Founded in 1880 by a group of avid canoeists, the ACA has grown into the nation's largest and most active nonprofit paddlesport organization. Today the ACA is dedicated to promoting canoeing, kayaking, and rafting as wholesome lifetime recreational activities, accomplishing this mission by providing a variety of worthwhile programs and public services in such areas as event sponsorship, safety education, instructor certification, waterway stewardship, development of water trails, paddlers' rights and protection, and public information campaigns.

Kayaking contains nine chapters covering the principles and techniques needed for safe and efficient kayaking. **Chapter 1** presents the history of kayaking as well as information on types of kayaking, outdoor ethics, and resources. **Chapter 2** includes fitness requirements for paddlers, including stretching, nutrition, and components of a training program. **Chapter 3** covers the equipment you will use while enjoying your kayaking adventure. **Chapter 4** gets you ready for your trip by detailing all aspects of trip planning, including pretrip planning, on-water management, and kayak ethics and etiquette. **Chapter 5** details safety aspects of paddlesports, whether you plan on being on a lake, pond, lazy river, challenging whitewater, or coastal waters. **Chapter 6** introduces the fundamental kayaking techniques, strokes, and maneuvers, including concepts of paddling and boat dynamics in the water. **Chapter 7** takes you to the sea and gives you the information you need to know to take your kayak on the coastal waters. **Chapter 8** takes you to the river in order to illustrate the dynamics of moving water as they relate to a river trip. **Chapter 9** provides excellent resources on sharing paddlesports with others through use and stewardship of resources, paddlers' environmental ethics, and further paddling opportunities.

In each of the chapters you will find safety tips, paddling tips, and consumer tips highlighting interesting and important facts to remember about kayaking. Diagrams and photographs illustrate the techniques and concepts explained in the text. In addition, there are checklists to help you get organized as you plan for an outing. The book concludes with lists of Web resources for additional information on each of the topics covered in the book and success checks to test your retention of the information provided in the chapters.

Kayaking also includes the *Quick Start Your Kayak* DVD, which guides you through an introduction to paddlesports and basic safety and paddling techniques so you can enjoy a safe boating experience.

We hope that you find *Kayaking* a valuable resource as you start your own on-water adventure or continue the one already started. Be safe, happy, and smart on the water.

Note: This text includes a wealth of information about the sport of kayaking, including techniques, on-water information, and trip planning. However, it is not designed as a replacement for effective on-water instruction. As you enjoy the sport of kayaking, it is important to search out and participate in on-water instruction by qualified instructors.

Acknowledgments

Thank you to the many individuals and members of the American Canoe Association Safety Education and Instruction Council who assisted in putting *Kayaking* together. You are too many to list, but your contributions were essential to the creation of this excellent resource to paddlers. With your expertise and input, we have created an invaluable resource for outdoor enthusiasts interested in paddlesports.

A special thank you to Dr. Chuck Sutherland for the use of his reference materials used in the development of the cold water shock and cold water immersion components of this book.

Additional thanks go to the following organizations for supporting this project: Northwest River Supplies, Frostburg State University, and Garrett College.

The *Quick Start Your Kayak* DVD provided with this book was produced under a grant from the Sport Fish Restoration and Boating Trust Fund administered by the U.S. Coast Guard.

PART I

Preparing for a Kayaking Adventure

CHAPTER 1

Going Kayaking

You rolling old river,
you changing old river,
Let's you and me, river,
run down to the sea.

Bill Staines, lyrics from "River"

L ike all my outdoor adventures, the journey started at home. I opened the storage room door and saw a collection of kayaks. My sea kayak was suspended from the ceiling, having been stored there after a recent trip to the awesome coastal waters of Maine. It carried me to reaches accessible only by water and into quiet coves and bays where birds and fish eyed me with great suspicion but ignored my quiet intrusion. My whitewater boat, now a few years old and in need of replacement, was propped against the wall along a chest of life jackets, paddles, and dry bags. Every scrape on the whitewater hull had been earned on voyages over challenging drops or watery sluices with friends in near proximity to share the excitement and fun. My fishing kayak was in the rafters and had seen great action the previous week with the neighborhood kids and my cousin's scout pack.

Today, I selected an old friend—my handmade wooden tandem touring kayak. Strapping it to my car roof racks, my journey today was closer to home. I would view birds and other wildlife on a local lake and introduce a new friend to the joy of messing around in a boat.

Overview of Kayaking

Kayaking originated as a means of transportation for native hunters, travelers, warriors, and traders. Early kayaks varied in design across parts of the world. Most likely the first kayaks were created in the Arctic region by the Inuit people. Used primarily for hunting and fishing, early kayaks were made with wooden frames and covered with sealskin. A hole in the middle of the craft provided a place for gear to be loaded and for the hunter to sit. Early paddle designs sometimes resembled a wide stick.

As the kayak was adopted by other cultures, the wooden frame was covered with fabric such as painted or treated canvas. Fiberglass boats came into use in the 1950s, with the first plastic kayak produced in the 1970s. Plastic kayaks generated widespread availability to paddlers and sparked an increase in levels of participation through the 1990s.

Kayakers today are primarily recreational paddlers (figure 1.1) but also include coastal (sea) kayakers and whitewater kayakers. Kayaks are still used for transportation, for tripping and wilderness camping, as an activity at camps, and for some, an athletic endeavor as athletes train and participate in competitive events.

This book gives you information on how to get started. It will serve as a complement to on-water instruction, but not a substitute for it. Before venturing out for your first adventure, get instruction from a certified kayaking instructor in flatwater, river, or coastal conditions. Under the guidance of a qualified instructor, you will quickly learn techniques that will keep you safe, comfortable, and injury free.

Figure 1.1 Kayakers can enjoy a broad range of recreational activities, including hobbies such as fishing.

Benefits of Kayaking

There are many benefits of kayaking—physiological, sociological, and psychological. Kayaking is a low-impact activity that strengthens the upper body. Paddling at a rate of 4 to 5 miles per hour (6.5 to 8 kilometers per hour) can expend up to 400 calories per hour. Kayaking lets you be outdoors and enjoy nature, and it is a great way to help the mind and body relax and unwind. Kayaking provides a healthy alternative for a fitness routine.

For those seeking social situations, kayaking provides an opportunity to paddle with friends and family. Many cities have paddling groups as a component of their local outdoor clubs, and outfitters schedule paddle demo days, day and overnight trips, and paddling instruction. River cleanup events help develop our outdoor ethics and provide a means to give back to the community.

As leisure time becomes more and more of a luxury, it is important to find activities that meet our psychological wellness needs. Kayaking provides an opportunity for personal growth in skill development and the achievement of new experiences. Personal values and identities develop from these experiences, as others recognize unique skills and abilities. Fitness, stress reduction, and social support are aspects available day to day or during a life crisis. Finally, kayaking is fun and pleasurable and contributes to your overall well-being, mentally and physically.

Where to Kayak

Nearly every water venue is suitable for kayaking. If you are new to the activity, begin on a sheltered flatwater pond or lake away from powerboat traffic, winds, or current. There you can develop a sense of balance in your boat and gain comfort in using the paddle and other gear. For many, flatwater kayaking on a small lake fulfills a need for adventure. Coves, historic bridges and piers, and cliffs and shoreline features on thousands of lakes and ponds offer an almost endless supply of sites to see and places to explore. Gaining confidence and experience in winds or water current expands your list of suitable waterways to coastal, Great Lakes, rivers, and seas. Lakes, reservoirs, large ponds, and quiet coastlines make good paddling venues for flatwater excursions. Many lakes have interesting outlets or inlets with nooks and crannies to explore, seek nature, or find fish. We will discuss the benefits of different paddling venues in future chapters.

Quiet Water (Novice)

A quiet-water lake, pond, or reservoir has relatively calm water with an almost glasslike surface (figure 1.2). A small body of water that is sheltered from the wind and has restrictions on motorboat traffic is ideal for the novice paddler. A protected shoreline and minimal boat traffic will minimize the waves created by wind or boat wake (the water turbulence that follows the boat as it moves through the water). Your safest route on a lake is along the shoreline, within safe swimming distance from shore. In the event of a capsize, you will be able to swim to shore with your kayak in tow and then reenter the boat.

Figure 1.2 Kayaking in a quiet lake is a safe route for the novice paddler.

A small 1- to 5-acre (.4 to 2 hectare) pond is large enough to practice paddle strokes, to fish, and to offer ample images to the photographer. The shoreline of a 650-acre, 3-mile-long (260 hectare, 5 kilometer long) lake could be explored in an afternoon, be paddled extensively for exercise, or be a great place for a family picnic—paddling, swimming, and a meal. A 10,000- acre, 15-mile-long (4,000 hectare, 24 kilometer long) lake attracts the traffic of larger boats, is more exposed to wind, and is less suitable for quiet-water kayaking, unless you are paddling short distances, along the shoreline, from a camp or cottage.

Gently Moving Water (Novice)

Rivers, canals, and large streams or creeks are often suitable for kayaking. What is the definition of gently moving water? A slow-moving river is one that you can paddle upstream, against the current, without much effort. It has little or no current and no riffles or rapids. It is not classified as moving water or whitewater (see chapter 8 for more information on river classifications). A river classified as Class I, the lowest classification of whitewater, may have some current and riffles but no obstructions or rapids.

Many people paddle a river using a there-and-back method; they paddle upstream for about an hour, turn around, and paddle back. Starting the paddle by heading upstream allows a less-strenuous return with the current. The water needs to be deep enough to float the kayak and to submerge the blade of the paddle completely, while clearing the bottom of the waterway. At a water depth of 3 to 6 inches (7.5 to 15 centimeters), kayaking is only fair, and you will find yourself getting out of the kayak to drag it through the shallows. A depth of 6 to 12 inches (15 to 30 centimeters) is good, and water 1 to 3 feet (30 to 90 centimeters) deep is excellent for kayaking a river.

Lake Inlets and Outlets (Novice to Advanced)

The marshy areas of lake inlets and outlets are often exceptional kayaking venues. An explorer can zigzag among reeds and lagoons, getting close enough to safely view birds, fish, and other aquatic wildlife from a safe and appropriate distance (figure 1.3). The relatively shallow water and narrowness of such waterways make access ideal for the kayaker. A word of caution: The boggy bottom of a marsh can sink a paddler thigh deep into muck, making reentry into a capsized kayak messy. Review the safety and survival skills outlined in chapter 5, and remember that safe practices suggest never paddling alone.

Open Lakes and Seas (Advanced)

Open lakes and seas are larger bodies of water. A kayak camping or tripping adventure often includes a passage through a large, open stretch of water. Open bodies of water are often gateways to quiet inlets or mouths of pristine rivers. Many beautiful island camping destinations are in the middle of larger waterways. Lakes exposed to wind are subject to waves, which vary in height and frequency with wind speed. Paddling in wind and waves requires endurance and efficient paddling technique. A well-trained tandem team can make paddling in wind and waves look almost effortless.

Whitewater (Advanced)

Rivers, creeks, and canals are subject to change as water levels rise and fall with change of season and precipitation. A gently flowing river can become a dangerous flooded waterway after a rainstorm. A lazy river that passes over a drop in elevation can become a raging field of rapids. For experienced moving-water kayakers, the challenge of a swiftly moving river is the adrenaline rush that makes them feel alive (figure 1.4) (see chapters 6 and 8 for more information about paddling rivers).

American Whitewater posts a national database of rivers and their classifications on its Web site (www.americanwhitewater.org). Some rivers are monitored by a regional streamkeeper, who updates water flow and offers paddling recommendations for the river. Many rivers and reservoirs are dammed, and dams may be subject to timed water releases. Paddling on a river below a dam can be life threatening because the flow and swiftness of the water can change rapidly after water is released.

Paddling Venue Resources

In your search for places to paddle, your best resource is local guides and experts. Retailers, clubs, and experienced paddlers can offer tips, recommendations, and guide services. Not all water is paddle friendly. Hazards—human

Figure 1.3 The shallow water of an inlet is ideal for kayaking.

Figure 1.4 Kayaking in a swiftly moving river with rapids and whitewater is an activity for those who are experienced and skilled.

SAFETY TIP

Motorboats: A Water Hazard

Motorboats create a water traffic hazard for the kayaker, and the frequency of boat traffic can be frustrating. Motorboats often use canals and rivers to gain access to larger waterways. Dodging boat traffic and dealing with wakes can be a challenge for the beginning kayaker. In large lakes, multiple boat wakes create a wavy cross-chop that is difficult to navigate. On canals and rivers, the wake of a single boat can range in height from 6 to 12 inches (15 to 30 centimeters). Wakes can be paddled through safely at an angle, but the unsuspecting kayaker whose kayak remains parallel to the wake may find the water rolling over the side of the kayak and swamping the boat. Respectful boaters will slow their speed to reduce the wake. When choosing your waterway, be aware of boater traffic patterns, and understand the rules of the road as they pertain to navigating local waterways. See chapter 4 for information about sharing waterways with other boats.

made or natural—are often unseen on a map and can be deadly. Be smart and check with the local experts before you venture out on your own (figure 1.5).

This book explores a number of ways to get information about paddling opportunities available in your area and around the world. A good place to begin your search is online at the American Canoe Association (ACA) Web site. ACA has created a directory of national water trails with information on how and where to travel, what you need, local contact information, and what you can expect to see on the water. Check out www.americancanoe.org for information on water trails in your area. You can search by state, click on a water trail, and in most cases find a link to more-detailed information. Some trails are designated as "ACA recommended," which means the waterway meets certain criteria making it a good destination for paddlers.

Guidebooks citing local paddle venues are great for reference. Many outdoor groups and local paddling experts (see the ACA Web site for lists of clubs) have documented written descriptions and classifications of their favorite paddles within a local geographic area. Experienced paddlers are your best resource for up-to-date water access recommendations, water ratings, and hazard references. You will learn much more about these topics in later chapters.

Figure 1.5 Novice paddlers should rely on experts for instruction and advice.

Types of Kayaking

Just as there are many places to kayak, there are many different styles of kayaking to accompany the location. Which style do you prefer? Sea kayaking, recreational kayaking, or coastal kayaking? Wilderness tripping or park and play? Touring, tripping, or camping? Slalom, sprint racing, or marathon racing competition?

The obvious question you may first ask yourself is "Do I want to kayak on whitewater, on coastal surge, or on flatwater?" You'll want a whitewater kayak for the first, a sea kayak for the coast; you have a number of choices for flatwater. There are even more subsets within these major categories. Details of kayak design and construction are found in chapter 3.

Recreational kayaking is one of the fastest-growing segments of the sport because of the ease in which new paddlers can obtain equipment, either through purchase or use of a rental or livery service. Families and individuals can paddle on small lakes and quiet rivers and simply enjoy a leisurely trip for the afternoon, maybe a picnic lunch, and time away from the hustle and bustle of everyday life.

Sea (coastal) kayaking takes the paddler to more-exposed open water, including large inland lakes and coastal environments, and can consist of short trips or multiday excursions. The coastal environment can require more expertise and experience, but it is a pristine setting where paddlers can visit many unique water and land features accessible only by kayak.

Whitewater kayaking—frothy rivers with paddlers in little boats, wearing helmets tempting fate as they challenge the river—is what many people associate with the sport of kayaking. This extreme image is not the typical whitewater kayaking experience. Whitewater kayaking includes paddling rivers with moderate flow and a few obstructions to high flow and very dynamic features. Paddling in such venues can be an art form because of the precision and skill needed.

Competition is very common in the sport of kayaking (figure 1.6). From the Olympic slalom to downriver racing and distance races, there are many opportunities to challenge one another and yourself.

CONSUMER TIP

Perform an Internet search for kayak rental businesses in your area. You can learn about types of boats available, places to go, qualifications to rent, prices, and so on. For a place to start, visit the Paddlesports Industry Association at www.paddlesportsindustry.org.

Figure 1.6 Competition kayaking is just one of many different types of kayaking.

Summary

Kayaking is the fastest-growing outdoor recreation sport and offers an opportunity to anyone looking for an on-water experience. Whether you are looking to float the local stream, challenge the rapids, or spend a week on the water, there is a type of kayaking for you.

With the ease of learning the sport, outdoor enthusiasts have embraced the opportunities. In this book, details of equipment, venues, safety, and technique will guide you to the type of kayaking that suits your wants and needs.

CHAPTER 2

Getting Fit
for Kayaking

The more specific your preparations, the better your performance.

Kent Ford

Spending time on the water may not be possible for you each day, but a daily physical fitness routine will greatly enhance each time you are on the water. Physical fitness is a crucial component of kayaking. Being physically fit goes beyond having enough energy to make it from the put-in to the take-out. Physical fitness means a safer activity for you and others around you. It can help prevent injury, and most of all it allows you to spend more time having fun!

If there should ever be a situation where a rescue is necessary, whether it's a capsize in open water or an unexpected swim through a deceiving rapid, self-rescue is the best method of recovery. Being physically fit enables you to better take care of yourself on the water and not have to rely on the skill and ability of those around you. Being fit enough to rescue yourself also means you are less of a risk and worry to the group you are with. It means you can more easily lend a hand to other paddlers in trouble.

As with any physical activity, injury is a reality. While there are some unavoidable and unforeseeable situations where injury occurs, most injuries can be prevented with proper paddling technique and physical fitness. Many accidents and injuries are a direct result of paddler fatigue. Being mentally exhausted can mean a poor decision when reading the river, and physical exhaustion could mean the current takes you places you had no intention of going.

Physical fitness is an integral component of a safe, injury-free, and most of all, fun kayaking experience.

Four Components of Physical Fitness

Before beginning a fitness program, you first need to evaluate your current level of physical fitness. Consult with a doctor to make sure your body is in appropriate shape to begin whatever program you choose. Deciding what program works best for you requires a basic understanding of what it means to be physically fit, and it is important to understand the components of physical fitness. Fitness comes in four varieties: strength, flexibility, endurance, and cardiorespiratory fitness. These four ingredients combined are a recipe for success on the water.

Strength

Strength is an unavoidable requirement for kayaking success, but it does not necessarily mean that bodybuilders will be better paddlers than marathon runners. Strength can mean different things to different paddlers, depending on what they want to get from their experience. Whitewater slalom racers and freestyle whitewater kayakers will need more brute strength than recreational paddlers or even marathon racers.

Flexibility

A paddler who is flexible is less likely to be injured than a paddler who is stiff and cannot easily adapt to a variety of circumstances. A flexible paddler is also more likely to last longer on the water and take more-efficient strokes. Torso

PADDLER TIP

Sitting in a Kayak

The kayak sitting position is not natural for most of us. Try this exercise to learn correct posture.

Wearing a comfortable and loose pair of pants, sit on the floor with your feet straight out in front of you. Lift your knees up and out to about 18 inches (45 centimeters) apart, with your heels touching and your big toes 12 inches (30 centimeters) apart. Place your hand on your lower back, and make sure that the angle of your back to the floor is 90 degrees. Your back should be straight, your chin up, and your chest slightly forward.

You should now be in the correct posture for successful kayaking. If this position is uncomfortable for you, it's probably because your hamstrings are tight. Practice flexibility exercises to stretch your hamstrings so you'll be comfortable in the boat.

rotation is a critical component of an efficient paddle stroke. The more you are able to rotate your torso, the longer the power phase of your stroke becomes, and the fewer strokes you need to take in order to cover a given distance.

Endurance

Most people can repeat a simple motion a few times without sacrificing technique or power, but the lasting repetition of those motions determines a person's endurance. The better a paddler's endurance, the longer that paddler can stay on the water without putting himself, or the group, at risk. The amount of endurance required depends on how much time you plan to spend on the water and how strenuous that time is going to be. Paddling downstream is much less difficult than paddling upstream, which requires a higher level of endurance.

Cardiorespiratory Fitness

Simply stated, cardiorespiratory fitness refers to how well the circulatory and respiratory systems are able to supply oxygen to skeletal muscles during sustained physical activity. If you have good cardiovascular health, your heart pumps with little effort, providing your body with the oxygen it requires in order to perform whatever task it is you are doing. If you have poor cardiovascular health, your heart must work harder, tiring more quickly and shortening the active portion of the task at hand. Cardiovascular health is not only a critical component in your steps toward becoming a physically fit kayaker but also a great way to reduce the risk of heart attack, heart disease, obesity, and a myriad of other health concerns.

A paddler's strength, flexibility, and endurance are dependent on how efficiently his or her body's circulatory system can distribute blood and oxygen to the parts of the body that need it most. This distribution of oxygen and energy is determined by a person's level of cardiovascular fitness. Without a steady flow of oxygen to the muscles and tissues, a paddler's strength, flexibility, and endurance will all be compromised.

Flexibility in and out of the Kayak

There has been a lot of discussion in the fitness community about whether or not you should warm up before you begin any sort of strenuous or physical activity. Again, this is the time to pay attention to your own body, how it behaves, and when it performs at optimal levels. Jumping jacks or a slow jog get the blood pumping through the muscles, but if your body tells you "no!" begin with a less-strenuous warm-up to increase your heart rate and get the blood pumping.

A good rule of thumb when stretching for kayaking is to work your way from head to toe. This way you can be sure you won't miss any key muscle groups. While you stretch, breathe deeply and consistently, holding your stretches for 10 to 15 seconds. Bouncing may allow you to touch your toes, but doing so may pull a muscle. Rather than touching your toes for a split second, gradually release tension in your muscles. Slowly relax your gluteal muscles, your hamstrings, and your calves until your toes are within reach. Consistent, proper stretching leads to increased flexibility—one of the four major components of good physical fitness.

Stretches From Head to Toe

There are many stretches for lots of muscle groups. While some work well for you, they may not be as effective for others. Listen to your body, and experiment. If it hurts, don't do it. Try another stretch that engages the same muscle group, and practice the routine before, and after, you paddle.

TECHNIQUE TIP

Use what's at hand to make stretching easier. Use a paddle for balance or as a lever against a stationary object to release tension.

Head and Neck

Paddling demands familiarity with your surroundings and understanding that those surroundings can quickly change. Keep your head on a swivel, but only do so after stretching. Press your ear toward your shoulder, and feel the stretch on the opposite side of the neck. Use your hand to press on your head to slowly increase the tension. Switch sides and repeat.

Shoulders

Shoulder injuries are typically a result of extending your arms where your body is not used to going. Keep your shoulders loose by doing arm circles. With your arms out to your side, parallel to the ground, draw circles in the air. Start out small, and then gradually increase the diameter. Reverse directions.

Chest

Power strokes engage the pectoral muscles while paddling. Place your hands behind your back, grab your own wrist, and slowly lift upward. Or, find a tree or buddy, hold your arm out to your side, palm pressing against the tree, and slowly turn your body outward, facing away from the tree or your buddy. Switch sides.

Back

Hold your arm out in front of you, and cross it over your chest. Using your other hand, squeeze your arm into your chest just above the elbow. Feel the stretch between your spine and shoulder blade.

Grab a partner and stand facing each other. Reach out and hold each other's wrists, then lean away from each other. Feel the stretch in your lower and upper back.

Biceps

Hold one arm out in front of you, palm facing up. With your other hand, grab your outstretched fingers from below and pull them down toward your body. Switch sides. This is also a great stretch to loosen your forearms if they tighten up after paddling long distances.

Triceps

Raise one arm above your head, then bending at the elbow, lower your forearm behind your head. With the other hand, grab your elbow and slowly pull so your fingers extend down your spine. Switch sides.

Core

If you are new to kayaking and you learn to paddle correctly, you will be amazed at how much your abdominal muscles, obliques, and ribs are engaged in the activity. These stretches allow for greater abdominal flexibility and rotation.

With your feet shoulder-width apart, place your hands on top of your head and slowly bend to one side, feeling the stretch along the other side of your body. Switch sides.

Next, place your hands on your hips and slowly bend backward at the waist so your chest faces the sky. Remember to breathe!

Groin

Stand with your feet far apart, slightly wider than your shoulders. Keeping your spine perpendicular to the ground, lunge to one side, keeping the opposite leg fairly straight. Feel the stretch on the inside of your straight leg. Switch sides.

Gluteal Muscles

Lie down on your back. Bend one leg at the knee and bring your knee to your chest, feeling the stretch just above your hamstring.

Quadriceps

While standing upright, bring your heel to your butt and hold at the ankle. Be sure to point your knee straight down at the ground while holding this stretch. Focus on a blade of grass to keep your balance, or use a paddle to support yourself.

Hamstrings

Stand with your feet a little farther than shoulder-width apart. Being careful not to lock your knees, bend forward at the waist. Grab both ankles, and pull your torso in to your legs to increase the intensity. Stand up, breathe, and then bend forward at the waist. Grab one ankle with both hands, and press your chest to your knee. Stand up and switch sides.

Calves

Begin on the ground on your hands and knees. Plant the balls of your feet on the ground, and slowly straighten your legs until your body forms an inverted "V."

Ankles

You never know when you will find yourself out of the kayak, scrambling over rocks and rough terrain. Paddlers are not immune to ankle sprains. Draw slow, wide circles in the air with your toes, rotating at the ankle. Change directions, and then switch feet.

Stretching in the Boat

We would all like to be flexible all the time, but our muscles will inevitably contract, especially after extended use. This muscle contraction can happen while you are paddling as well, but you may not have the luxury of pulling on shore to run through your routine. Discover ways to stretch while still in the kayak; just be sure to do so safely in a controlled environment.

Stretching after you get in the kayak not only increases your flexibility and reduces injury but also is a great way to test your range of motion while in the boat. Knowing your limits can be the difference between catching an eddy and pulling a muscle. While in the boat, simple techniques such as extending your legs in front of you and wiggling your toes will increase the blood flow.

While holding the paddle, rotate your torso to one side so that your paddle presses against the opposite bow, stretching your sides, abdominal muscles, and back (figure 2.1a). Bend at the waist and reach for the bow, or front, of the kayak, or the edge of the cockpit, and stretch out your back (figure 2.1b). Instead of holding on to a tree or buddy, reach one arm behind you and grab the back of the cockpit, rotate your torso toward the opposite side of the boat, and feel the stretch in your chest. Many of the upper-body exercises you performed on land can be done while in the boat. Be creative, stay limber, and stay hydrated.

Stretching After You Paddle

After a long day on the river, often all you want to think about is loading the boats and getting home. Although it may feel better at the time to sit and catch your breath, spend 15 minutes cooling down your muscles and stretching. While on the water you spent a lot of energy making the boat do what you wanted

Figure 2.1 Stretching in the kayak not only increases your flexibility, but it also allows you to test your range of motion while in the kayak.

it to do, and lactic acid has built up in your muscles. A postworkout stretch will make you feel better, and perform better, the next time you ask for extra output from your body. Simply repeat your prepaddle flexibility routine, but spend a bit more time on the muscles and joints that feel most sore.

Key Components of an Effective Training Program

There is no denying that being physically fit leads to a more successful paddling experience. The process of becoming physically fit and maintaining fitness levels can be fun and exciting. Lifting weights to exhaustion will not necessarily make you a better baseball hitter. It might make you stronger, but evaluating swing mechanics and spending time in the batting cage will make you a better hitter. Paddling is no different. Spending time in the gym will make you stronger and less susceptible to injury, but that is no comparison to spending time on the water. Wherever and however you decide to spend your training time, there are four components of an effective training program: action, quality, variety, and fun.

Action

No training program, no matter how intricate or intense, will be effective unless you actually do it. You could have all the weights, training equipment, and calorie monitors in the world, but unless you engage in a fitness program with regularity, success will be limited. A systematic approach works well for some, but a more laid back approach could work well for others. The key is discovering a method that works best for you.

Quality

Just because you train hard every day does not guarantee success. The quality of your workout can affect the outcome much more than the number of workouts you conduct. Conversely, overtraining without adequate rest for your muscles in between workouts can cause more damage than good. Find a balance that's right for you, and give targeted muscles at least 48 hours of rest between workouts.

Many people live busy, hectic lives, and finding time for a fitness program can be difficult. Targeted training, training that focuses on specific muscle groups, in this case those used when paddling, will earn you the best results. Get the most from the time you spend getting in shape by making sure your workouts are quality workouts. Conduct exercises precisely, and pay attention to how your body responds to the varying motions. This mantra holds true in the weight room and on the water.

Variety

Boredom can be a killer when it comes to fitness routines. If your workouts start to become stale, the likelihood that you will continue the activity declines. Switch it up. Pick new locations and activities to put some variety in your sessions. Instead of running on a treadmill, try going for a jog along the river. Play basketball instead of doing squats. Paddle backward rather than forward. Engage similar muscle groups by choosing different activities. By keeping your muscles guessing, they will grow stronger with greater flexibility, and at the same time you will stay sane.

Fun

Make sure you enjoy your workouts. Find a buddy and exercise together. Bring along a music player to add some life to your on-water workouts. The workouts will be more exciting, and you will be more likely to work out again on your next scheduled day. After all, paddling is supposed to be a fun activity; there is no reason you cannot have fun getting in shape, too. Remember, kayaking is a wet sport. If you bring your music player, be sure to have it protected in a waterproof container.

Cross-Training and Off-Season Training

Outdoor sports can be invigorating, but they are only as much fun as your body is willing to endure. Participating in outdoor activities already has a number of limiting factors including weather conditions, dependence on others, and the always nagging "time" factor. Being in good physical condition helps guarantee that when the clouds part and there's a chance to have some fun on the water, your body is just as willing as your mind.

Kayaking can sometimes be cumbersome to do alone, so you cannot always train while in the boat. Cross-training is a way to stay in shape while at the same time participating in some sports you have not yet enjoyed. Most cross-training activities include both cardiovascular and strength training, but there are a few sports that emphasize one or the other.

Cardiorespiratory Fitness

Cardiorespiratory fitness is crucial for any athlete. When training to enhance cardiovascular fitness and increase the flow of oxygen throughout your body, start slow. Build up some endurance first, and establish a baseline. Once you are comfortable with your current level of cardiovascular health, advance toward sprints and more-difficult workouts.

TECHNIQUE TIP

Know yourself. Understand your own tendencies in order to gain the most from your workout. Are you a morning person or an evening person? Do you enjoy a regimented schedule, or do you prefer impromptu activity? Understanding who you are can help while paving your own path toward physical fitness.

Swimming is an excellent alternative sport for paddlers (figure 2.2). Getting involved in kayaking is easy and requires little effort, but the ability to swim is very important, especially for those pursuing whitewater or coastal environments. Knowing how to swim, and how to swim while wearing your gear, is the best way to be safe. Swimming can do wonders for your level of fitness as well. This low-impact (meaning few jarring motions on your joints) aerobic activity builds strength, endurance, flexibility, and cardiovascular health. Whether in-season or off-season, swimming not only keeps you in shape but also prepares you for an unexpected capsize. If you happen to find yourself out of the boat, you will be more comfortable in the water, and self-rescue will be a breeze.

Muscular Fitness

Cardiorespiratory fitness is an important component of being able to paddle effectively, but so is muscular strength. Having strong muscles is important not only for enhanced performance, such as paddling up rapids, but also for reducing the likelihood of injury.

Figure 2.2 Besides improving your fitness level for kayaking, swimming for exercise also improves your ability to be safe on the water.

In-season, sprints while in the boat are a great way to build muscular strength. Try sprinting for 1 minute, then take a 2- or 3-minute rest, then sprint again. Continue this routine for approximately 30 minutes.

Off-season muscular training can do wonders not just for your paddling stroke but also for your health in general. You will find once-tiresome turning strokes a snap, you will travel farther under the power of a single forward stroke, and minor course and turning adjustments seem effortless.

The more muscle mass you have, the higher your metabolism will be, and the easier it will be for you to burn calories, lose weight, or maintain your ideal weight. Increasing your muscle mass and strength does not have to mean pumping iron at the gym. You just need to add some resistance to whatever activity you choose and exercise with enough intensity that you reach momentary muscle failure.

If you live near a sandy beach, run sprints on the beach rather than the pavement. Winter blues got you down? Go for a hike in the snow, or put on a pair of snowshoes. Whatever activity you choose, make sure you are challenging your body. Think about the message you are sending your body while you work out. Try to convince your body that it needs to be stronger and ready to repeat that performance when you call on it again.

Take your workout one step further by catering it to kayaking. Focus on twisting rotations of the torso, and pay a little more attention to the upper body. Go to the gym and try to mimic movements you would make on the water, only do so with weights. Be sure to balance your workout (e.g., chest and upper back, biceps and triceps, quadriceps and hamstrings, abdominals and lower back), not only to achieve symmetry in the way your body works but also to reduce injury.

Cable machines, or simply some elastic tubing, are great ways to simulate the paddling movement while on land with added resistance. Pull-ups and chin-ups are good exercises for paddlers since they focus on the biceps, triceps, and back muscles, which are regularly engaged during the paddling stroke. Push-ups work the triceps as well as the shoulders and chest, which are also engaged during many paddling strokes. Set up two chairs about shoulder-width apart, and slowly lower your body between the two, working your triceps and lower chest. There are lots of creative ways to build strength, both in the gym and at home.

The abdominal region contains an often ignored, but critical, muscle group. If you think about the movements you make, not just in kayaking but in everyday life, there are few that do not engage your abdominals. Washboard abdominal muscles are not a prerequisite for good paddling, but a strong core reduces the stress on other muscle groups, increases endurance, and reduces the risk of injury.

PADDLER TIP

Swimming is a great way to train for paddling. Try the backstroke or butterfly to focus on the powerful back muscles to cater your nautical workout to kayaking.

If there is magic
on this planet, it is
contained in water.

Loren Eiseley

For a more-challenging workout, train with a partner, or consider hiring a trainer or coach. This can be an excellent motivator to keep you working hard and to maximize the time you spend conditioning.

As you work in the off-season, keep your workouts simple but effective: four or five days a week, one hour per session. This routine, done properly and effectively, will put your body in a great position to grab the paddle and go as soon as the river is running.

Be careful not to overexert certain areas of your body. As you train, try to alternate muscle groups. An overworked muscle or tendon can lead to injury. Rather than train your entire body in one session, switch it up. Even better, change exercises and movements to keep your body guessing. Introducing new movements trains your body to respond favorably in unfavorable situations on the water.

There are lots of free resources available to help get you started. Do a search online (see the Web resources at the end of this book), check a book out at the library, ask a friend, or ask your doctor. People are getting more and more enthusiastic about physical fitness and are typically happy to offer advice.

Most important, decide what you want from kayaking, and determine what level of training is necessary in order to achieve those goals. Be selfish. Find a routine that fits *your* schedule, *your* goals, and *your* body. The end result is longer, more enjoyable, injury-free time on the water.

Nutrition

Kayaking requires effort, and effort requires energy. To maximize your time on the water, take a little time to understand the basics of nutrition. Understand, too, that different foods work best for different people. Think about the myriad of automobiles on the market. Some require diesel fuel, some premium gasoline, some regular. The point is that different engines need different fuel to run most efficiently, and the human body is no different. Experiment and find the fuel, or food, that makes you feel, and perform, the best.

There are six major nutrients essential not just for kayaking but also for healthy living: water, vitamins, minerals, proteins, carbohydrates, and fats. The balance of these six nutrients is decided by what activity you will be

PADDLER TIP

Enter to compete in a triathlon. The variety of sports will not only keep you interested in your workouts but help improve total body fitness as well. Then, during the paddling season, look for a paddling triathlon (bike, paddle, run), and let your hard work in the off-season take home the trophy.

asking your body to perform and how strenuous that activity is going to be. Nutrition is a complex science because "proper" nutrition is different for everyone. In addition, experts are constantly updating what you should eat and how much.

Generally, try to match the number of calories (energy) going into your body with the number of calories being burned. If you plan on working or paddling hard (e.g., attaining a set of rapids), you'll need more energy to complete the task at hand. If you plan on lounging in the bow on a lazy river, your body will require fewer calories. Unfortunately, proper nutrition is not as simple as calories in equal calories out. The quality of those calories is just as important. Minimize your intake of processed foods, and maximize your indulgence in fruits, vegetables, and whole grains. Treat your body like a finely tuned machine. Give it the best fuel possible, and drink plenty of water.

Staying energized and hydrated means you'll not only have more energy on the water but also be more alert. Kayaking requires a quick sense of judgment. Make proper nutrition a priority.

Nutrition for the Recreational Kayaker

The best thing you can do to stay properly energized and hydrated is to eat before you are hungry and drink before you are thirsty. Tarot card reading and seeing the future in a crystal ball may work for a few of us, but the truth is we just need to get good at guessing. If you wait to eat and drink until you feel the urge, it is a little too late because your body is already in deficit. Eat and drink often! Pack high-energy snacks such as peanuts, granola, raisins, sunflower seeds, and dried fruits. There are also a wide variety of energy bars available. Some taste great, while others taste like sandy chalk. Find the ones you like, and bring them along. These foods are not likely to spoil on the river, they taste good, and they keep your spirits high.

Proper hydration is absolutely essential, not just for your awareness on the water but also for the safety of the trip. Water is lost by sweating, urinating, defecating, and even breathing. Take whatever water you think you'll need, and then take a little more. Although it is possible to overhydrate, it's difficult to do. Drink just enough water so your urine runs clear. Secure water bottles

CONSUMER TIP

It's okay to have a few sweets while on the water, but beware of the sun. Chocolate lovers should substitute hard-shelled candy, such as M&Ms, for chocolate chips in their GORP (good old raisins and peanuts) to avoid a midafternoon meltdown.

to the decking of the kayak or within the cockpit with rope or straps in case you capsize (figure 2.3). Hydration packs that hold flexible water bladders are a great way to keep fluids in the body, too. Secure one below the deck or to your back for easy access.

Food and water won't do you much good unless you actually eat and drink it, so keep it accessible. Instead of stowing food at the bottom of a large bag, bring along a smaller bag and keep it within reach. This way, every time you look down, you will see a not-so-subtle reminder to keep snacking.

Figure 2.3 Staying hydrated is easier if you keep a water bottle accessible and secured inside the kayak in case you capsize.

Nutrition for the Competition Kayaker

Some paddlers decide to take their on-water experience to the next level and participate in local, regional, or even national competitions. Whomever you face and wherever that may be, proper nutrition is absolutely critical for a successful outcome.

Competitive paddlers take training and nutrition very seriously. They read articles and books on techniques and strategies. Some even hire trainers or consult with physicians to determine exactly how many calories they need and how often they need them. If competitive kayaking intrigues you, consult with a physician or personal trainer to develop a diet that will suit your needs best. A wide variety of online resources can help you calculate calories burned and even plan your diet for you; see the Web resources at the end of this book. Invest in a heart rate monitor to be sure you are training at optimal levels, and plan your diet accordingly. Remember, no one diet works well for everyone, so experiment and discover what works best for you and your body.

Relearn the Fundamentals

Remember back in grade school when teachers dressed in giant grape costumes and made you memorize the food pyramid (now called MyPyramid)? It wasn't all fun and games. Those teachers knew what they were talking about. Nutritionists today know even more than they did 20 or 30 years ago. The portion size and the levels of the pyramid may have changed a little, but the principles are still the same: Eat natural foods, eat a variety of foods, and keep fat intake to a minimum. Every sport has some basic fundamentals that the very best of athletes and coaches focus on. Learn the fundamentals of nutrition, and apply those basics to how you will be spending your time on the water.

Summary

Fitness and physical training are important components of successful performance in kayaking, but they should become part of your daily activities, too. As your kayaking skills progress and your taste for adventure increases, remember that your journey will last only as far as your body will take you. Pay attention to the four components of physical fitness (strength, flexibility, endurance, and cardiovascular fitness) to maximize your potential as a kayaker. Train appropriately, eat properly, and treat your body with respect.

CHAPTER 3

Kayaks, Paddles, and Gear

For she is such a
smart little craft,
Such a neat little,
sweet little craft.

*W.S. Gilbert, from the
opera* Ruddigore

Proper gear, including a boat and paddle suited for the type of water you will be kayaking, is essential for a fun, safe outing. This chapter takes you through how to select the gear you need in order to kayak, including how to dress.

Selecting Your Kayak

Hundreds of variations of kayaks are available today. How do you decide what type of kayak is right for you? In this section we'll define the parts of the kayak, discuss types of kayaks, and then cover the various design features. Having this knowledge will help you buy the right kayak for you.

Anatomy of a Kayak

Let's look at a few features of the boats a little more closely. Starting at the boat's ends, or bow (front) and stern (back), are grab loops or little handles that are part of the rescue towing system. They are necessary if you're pulling a friend to shore or to help you hold on to the boat in the event of a flip and a swim. On the deck, around the seat area, is the cockpit rim. The elastic cord of the spray skirt fits around the rim and around your waist to keep the water out. While running rapids or big swells, the spray skirt helps keep the water out of the boat.

Both sea kayaks and whitewater kayaks have a molded seat that shouldn't wobble. It should be placed close to the bottom of the boat. This position enhances stability and comfort as well as the amount of space remaining in the boat. Some boats have a back rest or backband that alleviates back strain and enables the proper sitting position.

Inside whitewater boats is a foam pillar that travels the length of the boat, adding stiffness to the deck and flotation to the boat. Flotation bags filled with air fit on either side of the walls to provide extra flotation in the event of a swim. A whitewater play boat generally carries minimal gear such as lunch, and a throw rope for rescue.

A sea kayak, or touring kayak as it is sometimes called, is often rigged with different accessories designed for the convenience of carrying gear on extended trips. The sea kayak is more frequently used as a touring boat, so there'll be hatches that allow you easy access to a lunch cooler or to spare clothes. These airtight and watertight hatches also provide flotation for the boat in the event of a swim. On the sea kayak's deck you'll find elastic ropes to store your rescue devices or your map for temporary storage (figure 3.1). For extended trips, paddlers often have a deck-mounted compass.

A kayak has foot braces (often called foot pegs) that are usually adjustable, thigh braces, and a seat. Check to make sure that each of these is working comfortably together for your good fit in the boat. Foam can easily be glued to the seat and thigh braces to enhance your fit and comfort.

Sea kayaks are typically 16 to 18 feet (4.9 to 5.5 meters) in length and sometimes have foot-operated rudders or fixed skegs that help with tracking (keeping the kayak traveling on a straight course). Rudders and skegs are designed to lift up to go over logs or weeds. Whitewater kayaks, in contrast, are short and turn so easily that a single stroke can spin them in a circle.

Figure 3.1   A sea kayak with hatches and deck storage.

STARTING OUT: BASIC BOATING EQUIPMENT

Kayak

- Match the craft to the desired activity and the paddler.
- Follow manufacturer's guidelines for boat use and care.
- Don't overload the boat.
- Take care of the boat—keep it clean, check for hull and hardware integrity, and make sure any damaged parts are repaired before heading out.

Life Jacket / Personal Flotation Device (PFD)

- Properly rated (according to weight) United States Coast Guard (USCG) approved life jackets are required for every person in the boat, and should be worn by everyone whenever they paddle.
- Life jackets need to be fitted and adjusted appropriately.
- Match the life jacket to the desired activity and the paddler.
- Capsizes and falls overboard are common among paddlers; wearing a life jacket dramatically reduces the risk of injury or death during such an event.

Paddle

- Match the paddle to the desired activity and the paddler.
- Follow manufacturer's guidelines for paddle care and use.

(continued)

(continued)

Other Equipment

- Wear clothing designed for weather and water conditions.
- Bring adequate food, water, and extra clothing.
- Use clothing and equipment (e.g., hats, sunblock, extra clothes) to reduce the risks of environmental problems such as hypothermia and sunburn.
- Match extra gear (e.g., helmets, emergency positioning indicator radio beacons [EPIRBs], VHF radios, flotation bags, spare paddles, navigation tools) to the paddler, the group, the environment and the desired activity.
- Carry appropriate rescue gear and learn how to use it.
- Navigation lights, distress signals, and sound signals may be required. Check with your local state boating officials to find out what you need to carry with you.

Kayak Parts and Nomenclature

An understanding of the parts of a kayak (figure 3.2) helps you determine what type of boat to use in specific paddling conditions. Knowing kayak and paddle parts is also useful when learning strokes and maneuvers or in communicating when paddling with others.

- Backband or seat back—The support structure in the seat to give lower back support.
- Beam—The width of the kayak at its widest point. A wider-beamed boat is more stable but slower to paddle.
- Bow—The front end of the kayak.
- Chine—The area of the hull where the bottom of the kayak turns up and becomes the sides.
- Cockpit—The area around the seat of the kayak.
- Deck—The top of the kayak.
- Draft—The depth of water required for the kayak to float. Draft is measured as the distance between the waterline and the bottom of the keel.
- Entry lines—The front part of the kayak that slices through the water.
- Foot brace—The point of contact for the feet. Sometimes used in conjunction with a rudder (sea kayak).
- Freeboard—The distance between the water-level and the deck of the kayak.
- Hull—The bottom of the kayak that displaces water and provides buoyancy.
- Keel—A structural or imaginary line that runs through the center of the boat from bow to stern. Keels are visible from the underside of the hull.

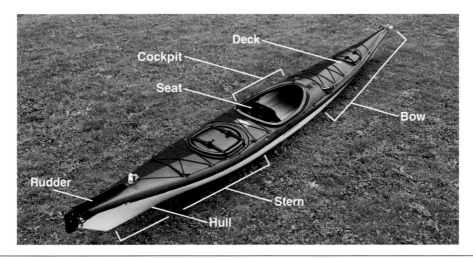

Figure 3.2 Parts of the kayak.

- Length—The greatest distance from the bow stem to the stern stem.

- Rocker—The upward sweep of the keel line toward the bow and stern. The more pronounced the rocker is, the easier the kayak is to turn. More rocker means faster turning and maneuverability. The trade-off is poorer tracking and more vulnerability to wind.

- Rudder or skeg—A mechanical aid to maintaining a straight path despite crossing winds and waves.

- Stern—The back end of the kayak. Most of the steering is done from the stern.

- Tandem—Like a tandem bicycle, a tandem kayak is built for two.

- Thigh brace—A point of contact for the paddler's thighs to help control the kayak.

Materials

The type of material the boat is built from is an important choice when you go out to select a boat. Two basic materials are used in kayaks today, plastic and fiberglass.

The plastic is generally a rotomolded plastic, not unlike the big plastic trash cans in front of your house or the plastic containers in your freezer. Plastic boats are thick and easily scratched, but most important, they are very durable. That trash can you've backed over in the driveway generally springs back into shape. The same is true for the plastic recreational kayaks on the market. (We are not recommending testing this feature!) The odds are that your first kayak will be a plastic boat.

For sea kayaking or whitewater racing, paddlers often upgrade to a composite boat, since the boat will rarely be abused on rocks. Composite boats are built with several layers of fabric woven of fiberglass, Kevlar, or carbon fiber material. These fabric layers are impregnated with an epoxy or resin that cures the boat to the shape of the mold. Regardless of which material is used, these boats are generically called composite, or simply "glass," boats. Fiberglass, Kevlar, and carbon fiber allow the manufacturer to mold finer lines to the boat and at the same time offer better abrasion resistance and a stiffer hull than a plastic boat. However, they do require a little bit more maintenance. You can identify Kevlar for its yellowish brown appearance and carbon for its black color. You can identify fiberglass boats by recognizing that they are built from two pieces—the hull and the deck—that are joined by a seam, often of a different color.

The fiberglass or Kevlar boats made with resins require more time in manufacture than plastic boats, and since they are handmade, these boats can be almost twice as expensive. You can feel the difference in rigidity and stiffness in the water, since the boat seems to glide faster and more easily. If you want the very best, very often that will be a composite boat built with Kevlar, fiberglass, and perhaps carbon. Particularly for sea kayaks, the lighter weight can be appealing.

Types of Kayaks

Imagine looking through a kayak buyer's guide to choose a boat and gear and discovering thousands of different boat designs and more than a hundred varieties of equipment. The number of styles and subtle differences in form and function can make your head spin. Fortunately, it is easy to narrow down the choices to a selection of gear that is well suited to the recreational paddler.

On one end of the kayak spectrum is a touring kayak. It is generally long (13 to 18 feet; 4 to 5.5 meters) and has a finer entry into the water. This shape helps it go straight easily. The bottom of the boat, called the hull, affects the tracking and turning characteristics of the boat, while the top, the deck, keeps the water out and helps the handling in big water. In contrast, whitewater play boats are fairly short (5 to 11 feet; 1.8 to 3.4 meters), somewhat broad, and have a blunt entry into the water, characteristics that make sense for spinning and dancing through waves and rapids.

Design Features

Kayak design is as varied as that for downhill skis or hiking boots. When deciding the type of kayak you want, be sure to consider how long your kayak should be for tracking or turning purposes; the stability of the craft, remembering that the more stable the kayak, typically the slower it is in the water; and finally how heavy it is. Will you be able to place the kayak on your car for transporting to and from the water? See table 3.1 for a chart to help you decide on what kind of kayak you need.

Table 3.1 What Kind of Kayak Do You Need?

Whitewater kayaks	
If your main use is:	**Then you'll want:**
Typical	Beginners play boat
Competition	Slalom kayak or downriver kayak
Fringe maneuvers	Squirt boat or play boat
Storage, transport key factors?	Inflatable
Large volume, steep creeks	Creek boat
Swimming pools, ponds	Polo boat
Touring kayaks	
If your main use is:	**Then you'll want:**
Typical	Day touring kayak
Warm climates	Sit-on-top boat
Multiday trips	Expedition boat
Kids to take?	Tandem boat
Historical fascination?	Aleut or Inuit designs
Storage, transport key factors?	Foldboat

Length and Width

The most basic variables in boat design are the length and width. All other things being equal, a longer, narrower boat will be faster than a shorter and wider boat. But the short, wide boat will turn more easily.

Remember that whitewater play boats are fairly short, somewhat broad, and have a blunt entry into the water. A sea kayak, in contrast, is generally much longer and has a finer entry into the water. The sea kayak and the whitewater play boat represent the two extremes of the design spectrum. Using this basic understanding of design, two different sea kayaks or two different whitewater play boats can be compared by eyeballing the length-to-width ratio. Also look at the entry point of the waterline at the very front of the boat. Is it sharp and knifelike or blunt like a spoon? The entry point can help you guess which will probably be the faster boat and which will probably turn the quickest.

Stability

Stability is another factor that is very important to paddlers evaluating boats. A boat that remains wide along its length will be more stable than a boat that widens only very briefly and then narrows again. Judging this is difficult because the width can be in different places relative to the waterline. Width above the waterline doesn't create a boat that is as stable as a boat that has a lot of width below the waterline. Paddlers have come up with terms describing types of stability: initial stability and secondary stability.

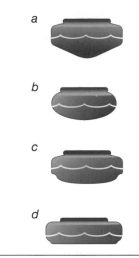

Figure 3.3 Various hull shapes: *(a)* V-hull of a touring kayak, *(b)* displacement hull of a whitewater kayak or the round hull of a touring kayak, *(c)* planing hull of a whitewater kayak, and *(d)* the flat bottom of a recreational kayak.

Initial stability occurs when the kayaker tries rocking the boat from side to side and the boat feels very secure, like a stable platform. Boats with a lot of initial stability generally have a very hard chine, or sharp corner on the hull. Boats with hard chines have a lot of initial stability and generally very little secondary stability. As you lean, the boat is stable up to a point, and then suddenly it will pass the point of stability and tip over.

Boats with solid secondary stability tend to have a rounder hull in the cross section. Those boats are not quite as stable when you first enter, but when rolled way up on their sides, they will still have a fair amount of stability. Generally speaking, you will want extra stability (meaning a wider, flatter hull) for general recreation and for diverse uses, such as photography. For racing and other sporting types of kayaking, you'll want a narrower, more responsive and demanding boat. See figure 3.3 for the different types of hull shapes.

Rocker

Rocker is another feature to consider when deciding what kind of kayak you want to buy. Rocker is the degree to which the hull curves at the ends. A boat that has a lot of rocker will spin more easily, while a boat that has little rocker will be faster. See figure 3.4 for different types of rocker.

Try Before You Buy

After you've decided what kind of kayak you want, narrow the field down to a few specific models by investigating the manufacturer exhibitions, demo days, symposiums, and paddle clubs. You can also line up with a professional school, where they have a variety of different boats that you can trade in and out of during the course of a day or two. Often touring kayaks are available for rental for day outings, but renting whitewater boats is hit or miss because many organizations are concerned about being sued if you get hurt. The likelihood of renting is better if you have taken a class from the organization.

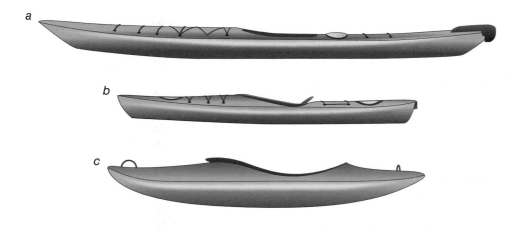

Figure 3.4 Rocker shapes vary by the type of kayak: *(a)* coastal, *(b)* recreational, and *(c)* whitewater. The whitewater kayak has the most rocker while the coastal kayak has the least.

Buying a used boat can be an affordable option, and a good rule of thumb is to look for boats that are in pretty good condition, with no major breaks. A boat that is less than five years old assures you of a design that's pretty far along in the evolution of the sport. Some of the older designs are less comfortable, so be especially careful that you fit the boat. Like most major capital expenditures, kayaks depreciate nearly 50 percent in the first year. After five years, the value of a kayak in good condition rarely drops to less than a third of its original retail price.

Get the Right Size

When you've settled on the type of boat you want, you'll need to consider how you fit specific boats. Boats now come in many sizes. In the earlier days of the sport, kayaks were pretty much built for big muscular guys and often didn't even fit them comfortably. Today, the ergonomics of outfitting is greatly improved, and now there are kayaks specifically designed for smaller people, particularly children and women.

The bucket seat of most kayaks is form-fitted to someone's butt, and that butt probably isn't like yours. If the seat has a sufficient forward angle, you should feel that it encourages you to sit up straight rather than slump in the boat. To find a boat that fits, start by finding a comfortable position on the floor to evaluate your flexibility. Are you comfortable sitting straight up with your legs extended in front? Can you easily lean forward with your knees slightly bent? This position is a very basic starting point for kayaking. We address flexibility more in chapter 2.

Outfitting the Kayak

The majority of paddlers look for items that make the boat more comfortable and easier to paddle or gadgets that make the trip safer. It is said that you wear a kayak, meaning it should fit the paddler. The following items should all be taken into consideration. Some will come with the kayak, depending on the model selected, while others are aftermarket items you will need to purchase.

- The seat needs to be comfortable and can be padded with foam to suit the paddler. A backband or back rest that provides adjustable support for the lower back while sitting upright is most favorable.
- Thigh bracing may be adjusted or padded to provide a controlled, snug fit, which allows for edging and rolling. A snug, but not tight, fit at the hips allows for best boat control.
- Foot braces or bulkheads should be adjusted for a controlled fit that allows the paddler to apply and release pressure at the back, knees, thighs, and feet.
- A spray skirt for those trained in the wet exit, with an easy-to-find grab loop.

Eventually, all things merge into one, and a river runs through it.
Norman Maclean

CONSUMER TIP

When you go into a shop to try a boat or when you check one out at a kayak clinic, don't just hop in the boat for a couple of seconds to decide the fit. You need to try the boat on as you would a fine pair of shoes. Take your time, and sit in the boat for a while to let the nuances appear. After sitting for 5 or 10 minutes, think about what parts of your body are complaining. Most boats include an adjustable backband to help you maintain correct paddling posture. Check to make sure the foot braces, thigh braces, and seat work well together. You can easily glue foam to the seat and thigh braces to improve the fit and comfort.

- A compass for touring and possibly a bilge pump. Some sea kayaks have these as options during construction.
- Optional deck bags, waterproof or not, for carrying gear on top of the boat for sea kayaks.
- Grab loops or toggles at the ends of the kayak for both carrying and rescue are pretty standard on all kayaks, and safety line around the deck is a necessity for sea kayaks.
- Reflective strips of tape that may be applied or factory installed for night visibility are suggested.

Life Jackets or Personal Flotation Devices

Personal flotation devices (PFDs) are commonly called life jackets. The law in most cases requires only that one PFD per occupant be in the kayak, but we say wear one properly anytime and all the time you are in or on your kayak. You want a snug fit for freedom of movement without allowing the life jacket to ride up off your shoulders when you are in the water. This is really important, as a life jacket that is too loose can make self-rescue much harder or can come off completely in the water. Most people who have drowned while boating were not wearing a life jacket.

Fit and Selection

Each of the various types of life jackets has an intended use. Fit is critical; life jacket size is based on chest measurement. Make sure your life jacket is the proper size, and wear it zipped, buckled, and cinched. When fitting a life jacket, loosen all the straps, slip on the vest, and zip or buckle it up. Tighten the straps, beginning at the waist belt, working up the sides, and saving the

PADDLER TIP

Transporting Your Boat

Once you have a boat, you'll need a way to get it to the river. The best way to do this is on top of your vehicle. Rarely are the roof racks that come on a vehicle appropriate for boats, but if your car has rain gutters it is easy to add a boat rack. Most bike or paddling stores sell racks that fit nicely on the car. When you tie down your boat, do it securely with ropes or webbing straps. Boats flying off cars at 55 miles per hour (88 kilometers per hour) are a serious hazard to other road users and a serious hazard to your equipment as well. The standard minimum is to tie across your boat on each of the two crossbars, and add a front (bow) line and a back (stern) line to the bumpers of your car.

- Drivers are responsible for the load on or towed by their vehicles.
- Use appropriate knots, ropes, and straps to secure your boat.
- Use appropriate racks or trailers for your boat.
- Consider using locks to secure your boat.

Be sure that your keys are secure. Place them in a secure bag or clip them into the kayak with a carabiner rather than risk losing them in the water. Additional detail on carrying kayaks and transportation is found in later chapters.

Kayaks correctly secured to a vehicle.

shoulder adjustments, if it has any, for last. A partner can help with the fitting process, cinching straps and tugging upward on the shoulders, checking to see whether the jacket rises above your head (figure 3.5). A well-fitted jacket is snug and does not rise above your head, but it is not so tight that it restricts your breathing. Be sure to cinch the jacket while standing, and then check for comfort in a seated position.

When shopping for a life jacket, fit it as described and then use mock paddle strokes to check for range of motion and freedom of movement. Take time to note the presence of (or, you hope, the lack of) chafing or rough spots along the armholes and sides. Also look to see how far up the jacket rides when you sit down. Some vests have deep V-necks to keep the chin from rubbing against zippers or buckles.

Although color is a personal choice, bright colored life jackets (orange, yellow, red) are more visible on the water.

Types of PFDs

Manufacturers are required to meet certain regulations to obtain USCG approval within the categories listed here. A comfortable choice for paddling is a type III PFD.

Type I: offshore life jacket. This type of PFD is usually found aboard ships at sea. A type I PFD is intended for extended use in rough, open water. Because of the design of the PFD, an unconscious person will usually be turned face up. This type of PFD is extremely bulky and uncomfortable for paddling.

Type II: nearshore buoyant vest. Designed for use in calm inland water near the shore where quick rescue is imminent, this is the classic PFD. The orange horse collar fits this category, as do other standard PFDs. They come in several sizes for children and adults. Some styles will turn an unconscious person face up. Type II PFDs are less expensive than type I PFDs, but they too are bulky and cumbersome for paddling.

Type III: flotation aid. Type III PFDs are the most comfortable type for paddling. The streamlined fit, large armholes, and variety of styles offer options for personal comfort and fit. An increased range of motion gives paddlers a sense of freedom. These vests are designed for quick rescue in inland water, where the wearer must be able to assume a face-up position in the water. Jackets are available in a variety of sizes for children, women, and men.

Type IV: throwable. These buoyant cushions and ring buoys are not USCG approved for use in kayaks. They are intended to be tossed to a swimmer who is already wearing a PFD.

Type V: special-use device. This category includes rescue vests, windsurfing vests, waterskiing vests, work vests, deck suits, and hybrid vests that may contain an inflatable bladder for added internal buoyancy. Some are designed to protect against hypothermia; other vests may offer freedom of movement or are specially designed for a particular sport.

Figure 3.5 *(a)* Adjusting for proper fit; *(b)* a properly fitted life jacket; *(c)* an improperly fitted life jacket.

Types III and V: inflatable devices. Inflatable jackets are comfortable to wear, highly visible when inflated, and turn most people face up faster than do traditional PFDs. The user wears the jacket deflated but can rapidly inflate it by pulling a tab on a cartridge of carbon dioxide. All inflatables also have a backup oral inflation valve. Inflatable vests are approved only for flatwater settings and are not to be used for whitewater paddling.

Other Features

Life jackets are not a one-size-fits-all product. The more comfortable the fit is, the greater the likelihood that the person will wear the life jacket. Look into specialty and optional features.

Flotation. The average adult requires 7 to 12 extra pounds (3.2 to 5.4 kilograms) of flotation to keep the head out of water. Vests for small children and infants provide 7 pounds (3.2 kilograms) of flotation. Children's vests must provide 11 pounds (5 kilograms) of flotation. Adults provide 16 to 21 pounds (7.3 to 9.5 kilograms). Check the tag inside the life jacket to see whether it meets USCG standards (figure 3.6b).

Women. Manufacturers have designed specialty jackets with princess seams, shorter waists, and fitted foam that conforms to a woman's shape.

Children. Children should always wear their life jackets on and around the water. Check the laws of your state for local requirements. Infant and toddler jackets often have a crotch strap, a flotation collar to keep the child's head out of water, and a grab loop to haul the wearer back into the boat.

Figure 3.6 *(a)* A well-fitted life jacket with *(b)* USCG approval label.

TECHNIQUE TIP

A properly fitting life jacket will feel snug but will not inhibit your breathing. The best way to test a life jacket is in the water, making sure that it stays low and snug around your torso and doesn't ride up.

A life jacket can be tested on land. After adjusting the side straps, the waist strap, and zipper, try tugging up at the shoulders. You shouldn't be able to lift the shoulders up past the middle of your ear. If you can raise them past the middle of your ear, then you may need a snugger adjustment or a smaller size.

Make sure your life jacket is sized properly so it will fit comfortably over layers of clothing. A wet suit, sweater, and paddling jacket are commonly worn on the water.

Optional Features

Consider the style of the life jacket. Modern vests offer many options, such as zippers, buckles, pullover or front-opening styles, ribs of foam panels, and mesh backs. The shape can be short and bulky or long and smooth.

Consider life jackets that have pockets and space for attachments. If you want a place to stash small items such as lip balm, a whistle, a knife, and bug repellent, look for a vest with zippered pockets and loops or rings. Mesh pockets drain better than nylon pockets. Some life jackets are specifically designed for fishing, with extra pockets, loops, and attachment points.

Maintaining Your Life Jacket

A well-maintained life jacket can last for years. Wear your vest instead of using it as a cushion, because sitting on it can compress the foam and decrease buoyancy. Rinse your life jacket and let it dry before you put it away, especially if you use it in salt water. Store your vest away from UV rays, which can damage the nylon. If your life jacket becomes sun-faded, ripped, or torn, it is no longer USCG approved, and you should dispose of it properly.

Selecting Your Paddle

Paddles, like kayaks, come in a variety of sizes, shapes, and materials. Unlike the kayak, a paddle can make or break a trip, because it is the paddler's connection between the body, the water, and the boat. You will be carrying your paddle for the entire trip, so comfort and performance are critical. Criteria for choosing a paddle include the type of paddling you will be doing, the weight and durability of the construction materials, the performance of the blade design and shape, and most important, the comfort and fit of the shaft.

Paddle Parts and Nomenclature

As with the kayak, it is important to know and understand the terminology associated with your equipment. Figure 3.7 shows a paddle with the various parts labeled. Descriptions of the parts of this vital piece of equipment follow.

- Blade—The wide, flat part of the paddle.
- Tip—The end of the blade, opposite the grip.
- Shaft—The long, tubelike part of the paddle between the grip and the blade. Shaft length varies according to the paddler's torso height and arm length, sitting or kneeling style, and position in the kayak (bow, stern, solo) as well as the beaminess (width) of the craft.
- Throat—The point where the blade meets the shaft. The shaft hand rests slightly above the throat of the paddle. An efficient paddle stroke will bury the blade in the water up to the throat. The throat is tapered to minimize resistance in the water.
- Power face—The side of the blade that catches the force of the water on a forward stroke. The power face is said to be loaded with the force of the water.
- Back face—Opposite the power face.

Paddle Materials

Paddles are predominately made of two materials: wood and synthetics such as plastic or composite materials. Wood paddles reward you with a delightful feel both in and out of the water. They respond with a softness and warmth in your hands. However, wood paddles require occasional varnishing and sanding. See figure 3.8 for various types of paddles.

Synthetic paddles have aluminum, fiberglass, or carbon fiber shafts. Their blades are usually plastic, fiberglass, or carbon fiber. They have a broad range in quality and cost. The least expensive ones can be unacceptably flexible and weak, while the best synthetic paddle can rival the finest wood paddle.

See table 3.2 for the advantages and disadvantages of each type of material.

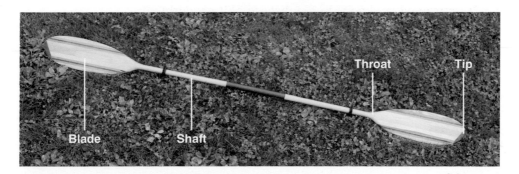

Figure 3.7 Parts of the paddle.

Figure 3.8 Various types of paddles including fiberglass, wood, and carbon fiber.

Sizing a Paddle

To size a paddle, hold it over your head with arms at right angles to the shaft (figure 3.9). Whitewater kayakers should have a fist width (4 to 5 inches; 10 to 12.5 centimeters) between their hands and the blades. Touring kayakers hold their hands slightly closer and have 5 to 10 inches (12.5 to 25 centimeters) between their hands and the blades. Additional consideration for paddle length should be taken into account. If you have a wider kayak, you may want a slightly longer paddle. Table 3.3 shows the correlation between height and arm span in relation to the paddle length. When shopping for a paddle, expect to find paddles sized in centimeters.

Small people should pay attention to the shaft's diameter. Most shafts are sized to fit the average male adult's hand. People with small hands, especially women and children, may want to order their paddles special to have a smaller blade and shaft diameter. If you experience wrist problems or mild tendinitis, your paddle might be the cause.

Paddle Designs

The paddle is what makes you go, controls your direction, and provides stability. Whether paddling a touring or whitewater boat, you will be taking about 50 strokes a minute, or 3,000 each hour, so weight and design are most important. This section looks at length, blade angles (straight versus indexed), and blade shape.

Table 3.2 Advantages and Disadvantages of Kayak Materials

Material	Advantage	Disadvantage
Wood	Delightful feel and aesthetics	Occasional maintenance
Fiberglass	Strength	Shaft shape and feel
Carbon	Lightweight	Fragile
Plastic	Inexpensive	Less-precise feel

Figure 3.9 One method of fitting a paddle.

In general, whitewater paddles and surf paddles are subjected to more stress than are touring paddles, so they need to be stronger and heavier by 6 ounces (170 grams) or more, which is a noticeable difference. Most paddles sold today have straight shafts, but a significant percentage have bent shafts, which may reduce wrist fatigue and allow a lighter grip, even though they are heavier and more costly. The decision is individual preference, with strong opinions on both sides.

Some companies also make paddle shafts of different diameters for those with smaller hands. There are smaller and larger paddle blades, with the mid-size fitting most people. Large blades are often used for fitness paddling and by most surf or whitewater paddlers, and smaller ones tend to be gentler on joints and may be more appropriate for smaller paddlers.

After shaft and blade size, look at blades designed for either low- or high-angle use. High angle is when the paddle shaft is held at a vertical angle of 45 degrees or greater, and low is less than 45 degrees as a rule of thumb (figure 3.10*b*). In general, whitewater and surf kayakers use high shaft angles to speed up their stroke rate and gain momentum in moving water conditions. Many touring paddlers use low shaft angles to keep the blades out of prevailing winds and allow for less-strenuous paddling for long distances (figure 3.10*a*). Again this is a personal preference that depends on paddling style.

Table 3.3 Determining Your Correct Paddle Length

Your height (and arm span)	Whitewater paddle length	Touring kayak paddle length
<5'2" (157 cm)	188-194 cm	210 cm
5'2"-5'6" (157-168 cm)	191-197 cm	220 cm
5'6"-5'10" (168-178 cm)	194-200 cm	220-230 cm
5'10"-6'6" (178-198 cm)	200-203 cm	230 cm

After you have chosen the paddle type, material, and sizing, determine whether you will paddle feathered (offset blades) or nonfeathered (same blade angle). Feathered blades allow the nonworking blade to cut through the wind at an angle, which reduces wind resistance. The angles also allow a paddler to use good torso

Figure 3.10 *(a)* Paddle shaft for low-angle use and *(b)* paddle shaft for high-angle use.

rotation when completing the forward stroke. Most whitewater paddlers use an offset of 15 to 45 degrees because of the faster cadence of the paddle strokes and less stress placed on the wrists; most touring paddlers use from 30 to 70 degrees to better slice through the wind. Many kayakers paddle nonfeathered and some with as much as a 90-degree feather. The larger the feather angle, the greater amount of wrist flexion necessary. This is another area where personal preference comes into play, and there are many opinions on what is best.

The traditional, or Greenland style, paddle has also become very popular because of its buoyancy (made from wood) and low profile, allowing for a very efficient and powerful paddle stroke.

Choosing the Proper Clothing and Accessories

Regardless of the clothing you wear, you'll get wet, be it from a paddle splash or a complete flip. The possibility of capsizing exists in all waters, and it happens when you least expect it. What's more important is staying warm after the splash or soak. Coldness can lead to hypothermia, which is life threatening.

Dressing for Success

Loose, quick-drying apparel is the best clothing for kayaking. Jackets should feel comfortably snug, but not so snug that they restrict torso movement while sitting. Choose roomy shorts and pants that don't bind when you sit. Synthetic materials dry quickly and will keep you warmer and more comfortable in the boat than will wool. Cotton can be used only in the hot summer months because once it's wet, it remains that way with no insulating ability. Even cotton underwear should be avoided. Most boaters wear a nylon swimsuit under their layers, even in cooler weather.

Be prepared for cooler temperatures, especially from wind on large bodies of water. And remember that water temperature, rather than air temperature, is the most important consideration. The typical temperature of spring runoff rivers,

PADDLER TIP

In addition to the most common straight shafts, some paddles have ergonomically designed or bent shafts, which proponents say provide better contact with the paddle and place less stress on joints and tendons. Bent shafts are generally more expensive and heavier than straight shafts of the same material.

lakes, and bays can be a frigid 40 degrees Fahrenheit (4 degrees Celsius), enough to rob you of your strength after a few minutes of immersion. It's wise to always be prepared for an unexpected swim. As you progress in the sport, you'll need to accumulate enough kayaking gear to protect you in a wide range of elements.

Layering and the Three Ws

The key to staying comfortable in the outdoors is dressing in layers. Commonly called "layering," the key is the order and function of the layers—wicking, warmth, and weather (see figure 3.11). The nice thing about layering is the layers can go on or come off as the weather or your body temperature changes. Dress in layers from neck to ankles for the most flexibility in controlling your body temperature during your outing.

• **Wicking.** The wicking layer is the first layer next to the skin. It is needed for moisture management and UV protection. Highly breathable wicking fabrics actually work to remove the moisture from the skin, through the fabric, and into the air. Choose a wicking short-sleeved T-shirt made from synthetic fabric

Figure 3.11 Layering: *(a)* base layer (wicking); *(b)* insulation (warmth); and *(c)* outer protection (weather).

SAFETY TIP

Hypothermia: Evaluate the Risk

Changes in precipitation or an unplanned capsize while kayaking can present the risk of hypothermia. Hypothermia is a condition brought on by a drop in body temperature after exposure to the elements. If the combined air plus water temperature is between 100 and 120 degrees Fahrenheit (38 and 49 degrees Celsius), there is a risk of hypothermia. Evaluate the risk, be prepared to be in the water, and dress accordingly. See chapter 5 for more details.

for warm weather, a long-sleeved synthetic shirt for colder days. You may also want to consider a wicking bra and wicking underwear. Some products also offer UV protection or bug protection woven into the fabric.

• **Warmth.** The second layer is your insulation layer. Wool, fleece, or pile works best. Most insulating fabrics are breathable and allow the moisture to move through the fabric. If the weather is too warm to wear your warmth layer, pack it in an accessible place so that you can retrieve it in the event of a change in temperature or an unanticipated swim. In cold weather, consider packing an extra or thicker warmth layer. Think about protecting yourself from head to toe by including a hat, shirt or pullover, gloves, pants, and socks.

• **Weather.** The third layer, or outer layer, protects you from the elements, keeping wind, rain, and splash water away from your body. There are degrees of comfort, protection, and of course, cost. Water-resistant breathable layers are worn to protect from the wind and will repel mild precipitation. A heavy rain will eventually soak through a water-resistant layer. The fabric is usually a tightly woven nylon, treated with a water-resistant coating on the outside.

Choosing Fabrics

Manufacturers offer an array of clothing and a variety of fabrics designed for the outdoors. Read fabric labels and hang tags to determine the functions and performance of the garment. Knowing the basics will help you select the right garment for your activity.

Cotton (e.g., T-shirts and jeans) is not recommended for paddling. It absorbs and retains moisture, takes too long to dry, and works to cool the body. Wet, cold, or damp cotton underwear is pretty uncomfortable too.

Wool is a longstanding outdoor fabric known for its insulating properties. Although it remains warm when wet, it gets extremely heavy and makes swimming or rescue difficult. There are new lightweight wool-blend fabrics available as an insulating layer that do not have the same weight concerns. Talk with your outdoor retailer for more information.

Spandex (Lycra) is a synthetic fabric made from rubber. Its major property is its ability to expand. It is found in most activewear, especially women's bathing suits and workout clothing. If Lycra gets wet, it will dry out when exposed to the sun. This is good for an underlying wicking layer.

Polyester refers to cloth woven from polyester fiber, a rage in the 1970s because of its no-wrinkle properties. Polyester fibers are often combined with cotton fibers, producing a cloth with some of the better properties of each. Synthetic fibers are a better choice than 100 percent cotton. Consider this for the wicking or warmth layer.

Fleece, or synthetic pile, was invented in the 1980s. Lighter than wool and more compressible, it maintains its insulating properties when wet. Woven from 100 percent polyester, using as much recycled plastic products as possible, basic fleece has evolved to fabrics that offer durability, warmth, breathability, wind resistance, odor resistance, and protection from the elements.

Fleece is woven in a variety of thicknesses. Microfleece is the lightest and is often found in linings of gloves or jackets. The 100-weight fabrics are about the weight of a sweatshirt. Medium-weight fleece, the 200 series, is probably the most common and versatile fleece on the market. The 300 series is designed for cold-weather wear. Wind Pro offers wind protection, blocking up to 95 percent of the wind.

The insulating properties of fleece are tremendous. When wet, fleece is warm, remains lightweight, and dries out relatively fast. To speed up the drying process, fleece can be wrung out and swung around your head. This fabric is especially good for the warmth layer.

Nylon fabrics are wind and water resistant. Some nylon fabrics are brushed to be as soft as cotton. Nylon is a good choice for shorts, pants, or a wind jacket.

Essential Clothing

The following items of clothing are essential, especially for cool-weather or cold-water paddling.

• **Pullover or Sweater.** A synthetic sweater or pullover provides extra insulation and sheds water when wet. Wool provides warmth but stays wet even though it wicks water away from the body. Some pullovers are made to wear specifically under paddling jackets, with a low-cut neck and shorter sleeves.

• **Farmer John Wet Suit.** Farmer John wet suit is the paddler's practical solution for cold-weather gear. Made of neoprene, it is a one-piece body suit with thigh- or calf-length legs and a sleeveless top. A zippered front allows easy access, while some have a Velcro or snap closure at the shoulder. The most popular thickness is 3/16 to 1/4 inch (4.8 to 6.4 millimeters).

The Farmer John is designed to get wet and provides some padding for those unfortunate swims in rocky waters. Its neoprene insulation works best when wet. By keeping a thin layer of water next to your skin, which heats to your body temperature, your warmth is maintained.

For beginning paddlers, the Farmer John wet suit is the best way to go in terms of warmth and durability. Perhaps the best combination for kayakers is the Farmer John and a synthetic sweater covered by a paddling jacket or a dry top.

• **Paddling Jacket.** A paddling jacket is made of coated nylon with neck and wrist cuffs to prevent water from dripping in the arms and upper body. Made of a windproof fabric, it contains your body heat. Paddling jackets generally are not waterproof, yet they can maintain a fair amount of heat if you've been soaked.

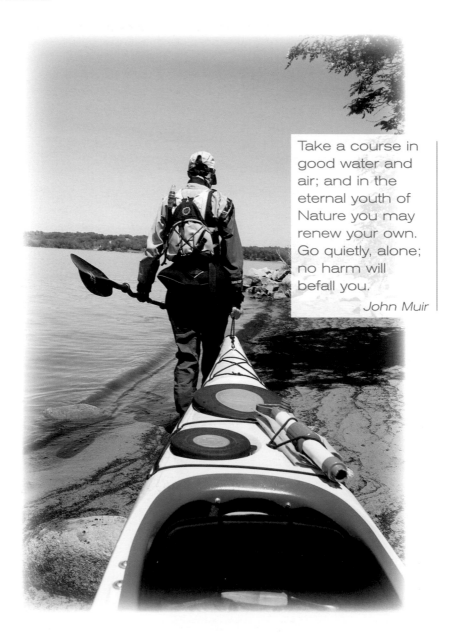

Take a course in good water and air; and in the eternal youth of Nature you may renew your own. Go quietly, alone; no harm will befall you.

John Muir

CONSUMER TIP

Synthetic fabrics are known by many different names: Duofold, Under Armour, Capilene, CoolMax, Supplex, Dryline, Polypro, Polartec, Synchilla, Polar Fleece, Gore-Tex, and so on.

- **Dry Top.** Dry tops are an alternative to paddling jackets. Most dry tops feature sealed neoprene wrist closures, a tight drawstring at the waist, and a very tight neck seal. The tight seals at wrist and neck are less comfortable, but the treated synthetic material eliminates all water getting in, keeping you dry. Although a dry top affords you the luxury of staying warm and dry, it doesn't offer much in comfort. Until it's broken in, the neck seal binds and constricts. After enough wear, the jacket feels comfortable, but the neck seal begins breaking down. Dry tops are generally more expensive than paddling jackets.

- **Dry Suit.** Dry suits resemble dry tops but have no seal at the waist and instead extend down the legs to ankle seals. Dry suits are great; if you end up swimming a bunch they can keep you dry. The disadvantage is again the discomfort of a tight neck gasket. Getting in and out of some of these suits is no easy chore.

- **Footwear.** Foot protection from litter on the shore or rocks on the river bottom is critical. A sturdy-soled shoe or sandal will not only prevent a foot injury but also enable you to run swiftly in the case of a loose boat's slipping downriver or a PFD's sudden flight with the wind. For those starting out in the summer season, an old pair of tennis shoes will do the trick. Ultimately, you'll want plastic sandals or neoprene booties that are specifically designed for paddling. They keep the sand out and your feet in better than most sandals or tennis shoes.

- **Headgear.** On almost 75 percent of your body, heat escapes through the head and neck. A wool hat is essential for staying warm on cold days whether you get wet or stay dry. On the coldest days, neoprene caps can save your life, especially in the event of a flip. A cheap but very workable alternative is a swimming cap combined with a wool hat.

Accessories and More Gear

Kayakers have a lot of gear to remember. Many a day has been ruined when a beginning paddler forgot some of his gear (figure 3.12). Even things such as a hat or visor, sunglasses, and water bottle are essential, and showing up with them at the start of your trip helps ensure you'll have a good day. What you should take depends on the paddling venue and length of the trip. See the end of the chapter for a comprehensive gear checklist.

Figure 3.12 A properly outfitted sea kayak.

Spray Skirt

Spray skirts that completely or partially fit around the kayak's cockpit combing are worn by kayakers on open water and whitewater venues for protection against sun, cold, and getting water in the kayak. *Wet-exit training is a must if they are to be worn.*

The spray skirt fits around your waist and the rim of the boat's cockpit. The skirt's elastic edge seals tightly to the rim. Generally the inside of the boat stays almost dry. Most paddlers use neoprene skirts that fit securely to keep water out effectively. Sea kayaking skirts are sometimes made of nylon, a material well suited for the boat's large cockpit and the weathering effects of salt water, but they aren't waterproof.

Spray skirts are sized to fit your waist and cockpit size. A skirt's pull cord remains in front and on top of the cockpit. A pull releases the skirt for a quick wet exit after a flip. This loop is a kayaker's rip cord. Even without pulling the cord, a spray skirt should not hold you in the boat against your will.

Helmet

Helmets protect your head. They should be worn when paddling in fast-moving rivers or surf conditions. They are a necessity when paddling whitewater. Helmets should fit snugly and cover your forehead and temples. Test the fit by moving the helmet with your hand—it should slightly move the skin on your forehead but not be so tight as to be uncomfortable. Stick with helmets designed for moving water to ensure that they drain water easily. Sea kayakers rarely wear helmets but should consider wearing them when they are exploring caves or messing around in rocky surf.

Sun Protection

A baseball cap or a hat with a wide brim helps protect against the sun. Because water reflects the sun's rays, almost doubling their effects, it's not surprising to hear the unprepared paddler complain of a headache.

Good-quality sunglasses help minimize the glare reflected off the water. Paddlers wearing contact lenses rather than glasses are at an advantage because they are free to switch their sunglasses on and off without interfering with their vision. Disposable lenses can work very well, even in whitewater.

First Aid Supplies

While carrying your boat to shore, you puncture your foot on a stick poking through the sand. Scrambling to shore after a flip, you scrape your calf on a rough rock. You cut your thumb while slicing cheese during a lunch stop. Injuries such as these, and they are not uncommon, can jeopardize your day of paddling. Don't let a lack of a first aid kit ruin your trip. First aid kits can be purchased, or you can develop your own kit based on your first aid skills and the remoteness of the paddling you will be doing. At the very least, your first aid kit should contain items for cuts, blisters, and allergic reactions. A more comprehensive kit is needed for longer and more-remote expeditions.

Tailor the amount of first aid gear to the size and needs of your group. Know the medical history of every group member, and check on everyone's current health before you leave on a tour, whether it's a day trip or a weeklong adventure. Find out if anyone in the group has a known allergy to bee stings, and if so, include an antihistamine kit. A quick exit off a lake or river, regardless of an injury, can be difficult and sometimes impossible.

Storage

A dry bag or a dry box serves as a waterproof container to protect your extra clothing and food. A small waterproof bag is useful for storing your sunscreen (an essential), lip balm (preferably the kind with sunscreen), your car keys and driver's license, and a first aid kit, depending on its size. A high-energy bar stashed in the ditty bag can give you a needed lift at the end of long day of paddling.

CONSUMER TIP

Read the label of weather-protective gear. The label will detail what materials are used to construct the garment and will also indicate the degree of water resistance. Waterproof breathable layers are designed to keep rain and splash water out yet allow the body's moisture and heat to pass through the fabric. Gore-Tex is a popular waterproof breathable fabric.

SAFETY TIP

The sun isn't always the cause of headaches. Sometimes it's not drinking enough water. Since kayakers engage in vigorous activity, their water needs are high, though often not noticed. If you are thirsty, then your body is a quart (or liter) low on fluids. Drink before you get thirsty to stay properly hydrated. A water bottle that can tie or clip into the boat within easy reach is a good hedge against a symptom of dehydration, a headache.

Rescue Gear and Safety Accessories

Flotation items, rescue gear, and emergency signaling devices are essential items to pack to help in rescue situations.

• Flotation for the kayak, such as inflatable air bags, is a necessity. Flotation aids are designed to displace water in the kayak in the event of a capsize and should be sufficient to keep the swamped boat afloat with you in or on it.

• Rescue gear such as a paddle float, sling, and pump for touring and a sling, prussiks, carabiners, pulleys, and a throw rope for whitewater. Tow rigs with 30 feet (9.1 meters) or more are common for sea kayaking, while 12 feet (3.7 meters) works on flatwater, and "cow tails" of 3 to 5 feet (.9 to 1.5 meters) are the norm for whitewater rescue jackets.

• Emergency signaling devices include items such as whistles, flares, flashlights, strobe lights, cell phones, signal mirrors, and VHF radios. For remote or wilderness travel, consider a personal locator beacon. The USCG requires that all paddlers carry an audible distress signal. The most commonly used and carried is a whistle.

Navigation aids, compass, Global Positioning Systems (GPS), maps, charts, and guidebooks can help keep you out of rescue situations.

Repair Kit

A repair kit should contain at least duct tape, nylon twine, a multitool or equivalent tools, and a knife. More-extensive trips need more-extensive repair kits.

Personal and Extra Items

An extra paddle is a must for any trip. Most spare paddles are at least two-piece paddles, and for whitewater trips, three- or four-piece paddles are made. For coastal kayaking the spare paddle is kept on the deck of the kayak, while spare paddles for whitewater kayaks are kept inside the boat.

CONSUMER TIP

Nobody needs to be a gearhead to enjoy kayaking. The basic equipment is required, and the same gear works well on most any water. However, the initial investment, depending on the type of paddling and necessary safety equipment, can vary from a few hundred dollars to more than $1,000 when all is added up.

Top-quality equipment is recommended for every paddler. If you need to cut corners, do it by buying a used boat. A used boat is easy to sell after a year or two. If you take a real liking to the sport, then it's time to upgrade.

Spare clothing that will fit most anyone and exposure gear such as storm capes, space blankets, or specialized shelters for when conditions warrant are generally carried in a dry bag.

Don't forget any personal items such as food, extra water, eyeglass straps, and bug repellent.

Summary

This chapter covers the technical nature of much of the equipment you can (or should) use when paddling a kayak. As your experience, skill level, and paddling venue change, more equipment may be necessary to maintain a safe and enjoyable trip. Simply grabbing a kayak, a couple of paddles, and a couple of life jackets is not sufficient. Be sure to take into account the many factors that will make the trip the best it can be.

Gear Checklist

Basic Kayaking Gear

☐ Boat

☐ Paddle or paddles

☐ Life jacket

☐ Signaling device (whistle, mirror, flares)

☐ Knife

☐ Throw line

*☐ Light

- [ ] Maps and guidebook
- *[ ] Compass
- *[ ] Weather radio
- *[ ] Two-way radio or cell phone

Personal Essentials

- [ ] Water
- [ ] Food or snack
- [ ] Sunscreen
- [ ] Hat
- [ ] Sunglasses
- [ ] Eyeglass straps
- [ ] Cold- and wet-weather gear
- *[ ] Change of clothing
- [ ] Water shoes or portage boots
- [ ] Paddling gloves
- [ ] Dry bags
- [ ] Bug spray
- [ ] Emergency blanket
- [ ] Matches or lighter

Shared Gear

- *[ ] Cooking equipment and kitchen items
- *[ ] Water purification system
- *[ ] Stove
- *[ ] Flashlight or lantern
- *[ ] Group first aid kit
- [ ] Rescue kit
- [ ] Food
- *[ ] Shelter
- *[ ] Portage wheels

Repair Kit

- ☐ Duct tape
- *☐ Extra bolts, nuts, and pins
- *☐ Screws and wood screws
- ☐ Multiuse tool
- *☐ Saw blade
- ☐ Plastic bags
- ☐ Epoxy adhesive
- ☐ Nylon cable ties
- *☐ Bailing wire
- *☐ Vinyl patch and cement
- *☐ Fiberglass repair kit
- *☐ Resin

First Aid Kit

First Aid Tools

- ☐ First aid manual
- ☐ Safety gloves
- ☐ CPR face shield
- ☐ Emergency blanket
- ☐ Magnifying glass
- ☐ Matches or lighter
- ☐ Tweezers
- ☐ Safety pins
- ☐ Razor blade
- ☐ Knife
- ☐ Scissors
- ☐ Thermometer
- ☐ Duct tape

* = for extended or prolonged outings

Bandages and Pads

☐ Band-Aids of various sizes

☐ Butterfly bandage

☐ Triangle bandage

☐ Large compress

☐ Gauze pads

☐ Gauze wrap

☐ Adhesive tape

☐ Moleskin

☐ Sam splint

Medications

☐ Antibiotic ointment

☐ Hydrocortisone cream

☐ Antiseptic wipes

☐ Non-aspirin tablets

☐ Aspirin

☐ Ibuprofen

☐ Antihistamine tablets

☐ Bee sting swabs

☐ Burn gel

☐ Calamine lotion

☐ Antibacterial soap

☐ Lip balm

☐ Bug spray

☐ Sunscreen

CHAPTER 4

Getting Ready to Kayak

Hang on to your paddle.
And if you hit any rocks,
don't hit 'em with your head.

*Deliverance, starring Burt
Reynolds, Jon Voight,
Ronny Cox, and Ned Beatty*

Prior planning is critical for ensuring a safe and successful trip. There are a number of additional things to keep in mind, including weather and water coupled with the skills and experience of the group. Extended trips require a higher level of planning and preparation. Remember, what you do not have with you on an outing could make a big difference in how the trip unfolds. There is much wisdom in the saying "Prior planning prevents poor performance."

Planning a Trip

If you are the trip leader, the first step in trip planning is to assess the skills of the group. Once you have determined each person's paddling abilities, you can make the rest of your plans accordingly. The route or the type of water you paddle needs to fit the group's collective skill level. Taking a first-time paddler along on a windy river trip will be frustrating for experienced paddlers and slow the entire group. A wide, lazy river or a quiet, protected lake would be a better option.

Paddler Skills and Experience

The kayaking event needs to be geared to the skill level of the weakest paddler. Answer the following questions to assess your group's ability.

- What prior paddling experiences have they had?
- Are there any similarities in experience among the group?
- What is the emotional commitment of the group (excited versus scared)?
- Are they novices, beginners, or advanced paddlers?
- Can they swim? Do they panic underwater?
- Have the group members practiced performing an assisted or self-rescue? Are they competent?
- Is anyone afraid of weather, water, bugs, water snakes, and so on?

Use the following skill-level classifications to determine the level of each group member.

- **First-time or amateur:** First-time paddlers or those who have recently been introduced to paddlesports. Experience and confidence levels are low.
- **Beginner:** Paddler can perform basic strokes to maneuver a boat in a straight line and avoid obstructions. Comfortable on quiet water and negotiating twists and turns on a gently moving river. Whitewater paddlers should be able to negotiate Class I rapids.
- **Intermediate:** Paddler is proficient in all basic and some advanced strokes. Paddler is able to safely maneuver in moderate wind and waves and can perform an assisted kayak-over-kayak rescue, T-rescue, and deep-water reentry. Whitewater paddlers can negotiate Class II to III rapids.

When you put your hand in a flowing stream, you touch the last that has gone before and the first of what is still to come.

Leonardo da Vinci

- **Advanced:** Paddler has solid paddling techniques and is able to perform self- and assisted rescues. Paddler is comfortable in large bodies of water, wind, and waves. Whitewater paddlers can paddle up to Class IV and V rapids. Coastal paddlers are able to paddle wave swells of 4 to 5 feet.

It is the trip leader's role to ensure the safety and success of every paddler. Do not put yourself or others at risk by making exceptions for paddlers who are enthusiastic but unskilled. Instead, rethink the trip so it meets the needs of the weakest paddler, or create a series of events to prepare people and build skill and competence levels.

Determining the Route

Once you have assessed the skill, experiences, and desires of the group, you will match these criteria with an appropriate waterway. Chapter 1 covers different water venues (quiet water, rivers and streams, whitewater, open lakes, and seas) and their appropriateness for the novice or advanced paddler.

As a trip leader, it is your responsibility to rate or know the difficulty of the route you choose. Experience is your best resource, and it is suggested that you be familiar with a route before you take others along with you. The trip difficulty is determined by the type of water you paddle, the length of the paddle (distance or time), and the number and length of carries (portages) included in the trip. Consult tables 4.1 and 4.2.

Note that precipitation, strong winds, and even heat can alter the difficulty of a well-planned trip. Alternative routes or time schedules should be part of your contingency plan to accommodate changes in weather. In the event of severe weather, you may need to cancel the event.

Table 4.1 Water Classification

Water type	Description
Flatwater	Protected from wind and waves. River, canal, or creek with negligible current, no rapids.
Open water	• Class 1: easy • Class 2: challenging • Class 3: difficult • Class 4: very difficult • Class 5: extreme • Class 6: life threatening
River classification	Rivers are given a difficulty rating under different conditions based on the force, flow, and difficulty of the moving water. • Class I: easy • Class II: novice • Class III: intermediate • Class IV: advanced • Class V: expert • Class VI: extreme Negotiating moving water requires experience with strokes, negotiating obstacles, and assisted and self-rescue. (See chapter 8 for more details on river paddling and classifications.)

Paddling guidebooks often rate the level of difficulty of outings. Check publication dates, making sure the information is current. Guidebooks may provide details for parking, lake or river access, and specifics about launches and take-out sites. The narrative description may help you determine whether a destination is appropriate for your intended group.

Local guides or experts can provide up-to-date information on water levels, hazards, human-made obstacles, launching and landing sites, and portage routes. Local guides may also be able to provide information on campsites, local attractions, and side trips.

You can search the Internet for current paddling or kayaking maps of your location. If there aren't any paddling-specific maps, a current topographic map, road atlas, or gazetteer is an adequate resource. Launch sites are noted by a boating icon, campsites with a tent or lean-to icon, and fishing access is indicated by a fish icon. Check the shoreline for public property that can be accessed for picnics or breaks (take-outs). Private property is to be respected and accessed only in extreme emergency or with prior permission.

Table 4.2 Trip Rating

Level	Length	Carries	Water classification
C	Less than 6 mi (10 km)	No carries	Flatwater
B	6-12 mi (10-20 km)	Short carries, less than .5 mi (.8 km)	Class I water—moving; moderate wind and wave exposure
A	12 mi (20 km) or more	Long carries, more than .5 mi (.8 km)	Class II water and above; moderate to heavy wind and wave exposure

Additional trip rating qualifiers

+ Trip will be more strenuous than a normal rating because of longer distances, open water, rapids, or carries.

− Trip will be less strenuous than a normal rating because of shorter distances, fewer classified rapids, or short carries.

Paddling clubs often maintain a local database of paddling destinations. The American Canoe Association (ACA) offers a national database that is up to date and provides reputable information for the trip planner. The ACA Web site, www.americancanoe.org, publishes links to ACA-approved water trails. ACA-recommended water trails meet a set of basic criteria and stand out as particularly good destinations for paddlers. To be eligible, a trail must meet the following requirements:

- The trail must be a contiguous or semicontiguous waterway or series of waterways that is open to recreational use by paddlers.
- The trail must have public access points for paddlers.
- The trail must be covered by a map, guide, signage, or Web site that is of reasonable quality and detail and available to the public.
- Published or printed materials for the trail (e.g., guidebook, map, signs, Web site) must communicate low-impact ethics to trail users.
- The trail must be supported or managed by one or more organizations.

ACA-recommended water trails earn the right to use a special ACA logo in maps, signs, and other printed material related to the trails. They also receive special recognition in the ACA's water trails database. The ACA names a new group of recommended trails during the summer of each year.

Maps, Charts, and Local Knowledge

Maps of areas are a good start for deciding first where to paddle generally and then more specifically. They show proximity to access (put-ins), take-outs, towns, parks, and roads, for launching, landing emergencies, and more. Topographic maps, commonly called topo maps, are often valuable to determine camping and hiking possibilities as well as exposure to wind and sun.

Charts, which are maps of the water, show water depths, buoys, day beacons, lighthouses, and other aids to navigation as well as shoreline and bottom makeup and often tide and current information. They also provide information for plotting a course and finding positions. Charts for paddlers need to be of a scale that shows enough detail to be useful for launching and landing as well as avoiding hazards—usually a 40,000 scale on the topographic map.

Navigation is a very important part of sea kayaking requiring significant study. Knowing how to use a compass and other navigational aids such as course plotters and GPS is very valuable. You should read and study the nautical rules of the road for interaction with power-driven craft before embarking on waterways shared with powerboat traffic. For specifics on navigation rules, visit the United States Coast Guard Web site at www.navcen.uscg.gov/mwv/navrules/rotr_online.htm.

Guidebooks and water trails materials usually are very helpful in determining the difficulty and time involved as well as features and hazards for paddling trips. Local knowledge is invaluable because waterways seldom stay the same for long—features change and hazards come and go. Find a local resource that should have current information and ask. Boat liveries, canoe and kayak shops, fishing equipment stores, and marinas are some examples of where to find local knowledge.

Float Plan

Once you have planned your trip, write down the details and file the plan with a friend, a ranger, or family member. Include details about the route; starting, stopping, and camping points; final destination; estimated departure and arrival times; and list of participants. Contact your designated person when the trip has ended, and agree to a plan if your contact does not hear from you in a designated time frame.

Pre-Event Planning Meeting

Before you hit the water, you will need to plan your trip in as much detail as the trip leader sees fit. This process of planning starts with the pre-event planning meeting, where the base for the trip and specifics of what and who will be needed are established.

SAFETY TIP

If you are traveling in remote areas, be sure to get contact information for rangers, emergency facilities, or civilized areas in the event of an emergency.

Emergency Plans

An emergency action plan (EAP) should be discussed if there is a possibility of severe weather (e.g., lightning) or if a potential medical emergency (e.g., bee allergy) exists among the group. Knowing these small but very important factors allows the group to understand the safety aspects for everyone while on the water, and the trip leader(s) will be prepared for any unexpected situation that may arise. EAPs should include but not be limited to the following:

- Weather plans
- Medical issues of participants
- Evacuation plans
- Local contacts for emergencies

Individual Paddling Roles

Beyond the roles of trip planner, first aid, repairman or handyman, meal planning, camp equipment, and gear inventory, there are four safety roles that are to be assigned to the group for the on-water segments of the trip: leader(s), sweep, rescue, and group. The roles can be explained and assigned at the pre-event meeting and later restated and clarified before the launch for a day trip. Similar to sitting in the exit seat on an airplane, be sure the individuals accepting roles understand them, are willing to execute the roles for the entire trip without distractions, and are trained and capable to fulfill the responsibilities of the roles.

Trip Leader

The trip leader organizes the final aspects of the trip, assesses skill levels, enforces water safety, performs gear and equipment checks, and is the person in charge of on-water situations. The leader must carry the map, compass, safety and rescue gear, extra paddle, and repair kit. The leader sets the pace and determines the route throughout the paddle. The leader initiates communication and river signals for the group (see chapter 5).

If anyone in the group has medical, physical, or emotional limitations, these should be shared with the trip leader and one other responsible member of the group. The leader needs to designate a qualified assistant who would act on his behalf in the event that the leader requires emergency or rescue assistance.

Sweep

The sweep boat brings up the rear, often encouraging and motivating weaker paddlers. The key function is making sure no one gets left behind. The sweep should be a strong paddler, trained and competent in rescue procedures.

Rescue

The rescue role is something that all trip members should be prepared to fill. The two boats closest to the troubled paddler should respond first. Rescue priorities are in this order: people, boat, and then gear. The remaining paddlers should gather nearby and assist as necessary without interfering. Rescue techniques are described in detail in chapter 5.

Group

The paddlers need to understand that they are part of a group, are expected to adhere to the guidelines set forth by the leader, and are to remain part of the group throughout the paddle. Communication, keeping eyes open for obstacles and hazards, and practicing safety and personal responsibility will influence the success of the trip.

Day of the Trip

Now that the planning stages are complete, it is time to get to the put-in and have a great day on the water. Even though the main planning stages are complete, the safety planning, preparation, and execution continue until everyone is back home safe and sound.

Wind, Weather, Water

On the day of the trip, reassess the safety conditions and decide if the trip should still take place. If so, determine how far you should travel. A well-thought-out plan for the statement "What if the weather . . ." will aid in your quick and safe response to changing circumstances. Wind, weather, and water are the major factors to consider.

- **Wind:** What is the strength and direction of the wind? Will you be protected from the wind? Will you be paddling into or against the wind? How much will the wind slow you down; can you make your destination by dark?

- **Weather:** Evaluate current and predicted weather conditions. Are you prepared to ride out a storm? What are alternative take-out sites in the event of an emergency? Will there be shelter available?

- **Water:** Assess water temperature; the size of the waves; and the strength of any current, rapids, or tides. Are water levels too high or too low? Have storms come through the area, felling trees and creating river hazards?

Assess the paddlers' skills against the environmental conditions. If there is any doubt about safety, it is best to either postpone the trip until conditions improve or until the paddlers involved gain the necessary skills and experience to successfully participate or select an easier venue.

Prelaunch Meeting

Gather the group and share the day's itinerary, including breaks and lunch times (see figure 4.1). Review the route, highlighting known hazards, emergency shelters or take-outs, and the end goal or take-out. Discuss skill levels of the group, including swimming ability and medical conditions. Designate or clarify trip leaders, the sweep boat, and emergency and first aid plans.

Figure 4.1 A prelaunch meeting gives the group an opportunity to review the route, the plans for the day, and any known risk factors.

Gear Check

Before launching, conduct a gear check (figure 4.2). Make sure everyone has the basics—life jackets, paddles, food and water, extra clothing, and gear for inclement weather. Trip leaders are responsible for carrying maps and guides, a compass, first aid kits, and safety and rescue gear. This is where your personalized gear checklist from chapter 3 will come in handy.

When paddling as a group, you can lighten individual loads by divvying up the gear list from chapter 3. Each person is responsible for her own basic kayak gear and personal essentials. The first aid kit, repair kit, and other items on the shared equipment list can be split across the group. The person with the highest level of first aid certification should be assigned one of the first aid kits, and the handyman gets the repair kit.

As far as the rest of the equipment, see who has brought additional safety gear and who will carry some of the group equipment. Pick the best and leave the rest. Make sure all your bases are covered.

Figure 4.2 Conduct a gear check before launching your kayak.

Check the boats to be sure gear is appropriately stowed and tied down. Is each boat trim (floating level) in the water? If not, adjust gear or people to see that the boat is loaded and weighted properly.

Sharing the Waterways

Just like driving and navigating highways, there are rules and rights of passage for navigating waterways. It is your responsibility to know the navigation rules for the waterways you paddle.

Be Aware

Always assume that other boaters do not see you. Kayaks do not show up on radar, and they get lost on the horizon. Large motor craft are not as maneuverable and have long stopping distances. Be aware, and use your ability to stop or get out of the way.

TECHNIQUE TIP

It is easier to plan a complete meal for the whole group than to pack breakfast, lunch, and dinners for each person. For extended day trips, meal responsibility can be divided among the group, just be sure you (or whoever is assigned cooking equipment) have all the cooking utensils and ingredients necessary to prepare your meal. For day trips, potluck style makes for an interesting meal.

Collision Course

To determine a collision course with another boat, take and hold a bearing off your bow. If the bearing changes as the range in distance decreases, you are not on a collision course. If the bearing stays constant as the other boat gets closer, you are on course for a collision. You should change course, stop, or do whatever it takes to get out of the way and let the boat pass. Use a signal device (horn or mirror) if necessary.

Right of Passage

Channels are marked for larger boats with buoys and red or green lights (figure 4.3). If you stay between the shoreline and the buoys, you are less apt to encounter wakes and traffic. If you need to cross a channel, do it as a group, not as a long line of stragglers.

Many harbors, bridges, dams, and drinking water supplies have restricted access and may be patrolled. Respect the authorities, and report any suspicious activities.

Paddling at Night

If you are paddling between sunset and sunrise or under conditions of limited visibility (e.g., fog, rain, haze) you must carry a visible white flare-up light to be shown in adequate time to prevent a collision. A bright flashlight or head lamp is adequate for this federal and state requirement. Shine the light in the direction of any oncoming motorized traffic to warn them of your position. Motorized craft have a red light portside (bow left) and a green light starboard (bow right) and a white stern light. The position of the lights help you determine which way the motorboat is traveling.

Figure 4.3 Buoys delineate channels for larger boats. By staying outside the buoys, closer to the shore, kayaks can avoid traffic and wakes.

PADDLERS AND THE LAW

Know and follow all local, state, and federal laws. These laws may include launch permits or fees, state boat registration requirements, and zoning regulations of certain waterways. Check with the local authorities before launching your boat on the water.

Registration and Education

Boat registration and education laws vary from state to state. Make sure you know the requirements that apply in the area you're paddling.

Local Rules

- Be sure to follow any rules or laws that apply to access and use of a waterway.
- Obey all applicable local, state, and federal regulations.
- Boats with motors or sails have requirements that can be very different from hand-powered craft—be sure you know what your boat requires.

Operator Responsibilities

- Boaters are responsible for their actions. Be polite and respectful of others on and around the water.
- Avoid large vessels and navigable channels, where large boats may have restricted mobility.
- Stay well away from military and law enforcement vessels unless they direct you to approach.
- Follow all marine and aquatic environmental laws—don't ask others to paddle in your trash.

Kayak Etiquette and Ethics

You can maximize safety and minimize social and environmental impacts by adhering to the following guidelines.

Safety Guidelines

Adherence to these practices will minimize potential personal risk and risk to others.

- Wear your PFD—on, zipped or buckled, and cinched.
- Avoid drug and alcohol use while kayaking.
- Paddle with a friend—never alone. File a float plan.
- Avoid a capsize!
  - Don't overload the kayak with people or gear.
  - Remain seated. Do not stand in a kayak.

SAFETY TIP

On extended trips, pack two stoves and two water purification systems. If something happens to one, you have a backup.

- Paddle in control. Be able to steer and control the speed and direction of the kayak.
- Leave space between yourself and other paddlers.
- Know your limits. Paddle in situations at or below your skill level.
- Be a competent swimmer. Practice swimming in your PFD.
- Know how to perform self-rescues and rescues to assist others.
- Dress for changing weather conditions.
- Keep an eye out for water hazards, and alert others to them.
- Know how to read the signs of changes in weather and water, and respond accordingly.
- Know and adhere to land and water regulations in your area.
- Be familiar with the rules for sharing waterways with other boat traffic.

Social Guidelines

Adherence to these practices will minimize the impact our presence has on the privacy and personal enjoyment of outdoor resources by others.

- Respect private property.
- Don't be noisy when encountering others on the water.
- Give fishers and swimmers a wide berth.
- Change clothes privately.

Environmental Guidelines

Adherence to these practices will preserve and protect our natural resources, ensuring that green and blue spaces will be available for future generations.

- Participate in local river clean-up days.
- Bring a garbage bag, and collect litter along your route.
- Practice water conservation at home.
- Avoid the introduction of invasive species.
- Use environmentally friendly products on the hull of your boat.
- Properly dispose of waste, including human waste.

- Protect shorelines by treading lightly and spreading the foot and boat traffic on land to keep plants and wildlife intact, which aids in reducing shoreline erosion.

Summary

Indeed, "prior planning prevents poor performance." Proper gear, attention to weather and water conditions, prepared participants—both mentally and physically—and a suitable level of skill all help ensure a successful trip. Prior preparation and attention to detail are important. What you do not have with you on an outing, both physically and in your knowledge banks, could make a big difference in how the trip unfolds.

Planning Your Trip

Anticipated Destination

☐ Match the paddler's skill with the planned destination—it's important for new paddlers to be conservative and choose paddling venues with minimal hazards.

☐ Check for weather and water conditions.

☐ Learn about local hazards.

☐ Learn about access points.

☐ Have a backup plan.

☐ Develop and file an appropriate float plan for your trip, describing access, length of trip, when you would be overdue, and what to do if you are overdue.

Equipment

☐ Make sure you have appropriate equipment for your type of boat and the area you plan to paddle.

☐ Make sure your equipment is in good working order before you head out.

☐ Make sure you have appropriate charts, maps, and directions.

Group

☐ Paddling with a group is safer.

☐ Ensure each group member has appropriate knowledge, skills, and equipment for the trip.

CHAPTER 5

Water Safety and Survival Skills

There is no such thing as bad weather, only bad clothes.

Old Norwegian adage

It was going to be a short, relaxing trip. Seth and Alex were eager to try out their new kayak, so they packed only a few items, making sure they had their new paddles and life jackets. They headed to Grand Lake, launching on the western shore. The late-day temperature was rising fast, and Seth and Alex did not notice the buildup of dark clouds behind them. Soon the easterly wind was pushing them farther into the open water, much faster then their new paddling abilities could handle. When the thunderstorm erupted, they found themselves scared, cold, and panicked in the lightning and hard rain. They laid low in the bottom of their tandem kayak to keep from capsizing. Strong winds pushed them past the warning buoys and toward the overflow of the Grand Lake dam. Not knowing what else to do, they dove into the 60-degree Fahrenheit (16 degree Celsius) water and swam to the anchored warning buoy, away from the danger of the dam. From the water, they watched the wind accelerate their kayak, blowing it over the rim of the overflow. They huddled together for warmth while awaiting rescue.

Know Your Boating Abilities and the Waters

Paddling in moving water requires special skill and knowledge. Good boat control on a lake or river is mastered through knowledge of the various forces involved and the application of those forces in a given situation. Your movement with wind or river current could cause you to come upon obstacles too fast to react in time. By knowing the proper strokes and maneuvers, you can slow your speed and assess the situation so that you can stay out of harm's way.

Paddling in rapidly moving water or high wind is a complex skill that requires extensive knowledge of the boat and the power of the water. If you are not experienced in boat handling under these conditions, you should obtain training and travel with someone who is. Through that person's experience; your observation; and your study of the characteristics of wind, waves, and moving water, you will soon be able to paddle with confidence.

"Know before you go." This slogan means you should read guidebooks, check with outfitters, or talk with paddlers who have experience on the river that you intend to paddle. You'll need to know about hazards, difficulty, water levels, the locations of put-ins and take-outs, and more. Make sure everyone in your group has the skills appropriate for the river or lake you intend to paddle. Formulate a float plan, and leave a copy with a friend, family member, or other responsible party.

Learn to recognize potential hazards, and use good judgment to avoid them. Inclement weather, floodwaters, and natural or human-made obstructions are all danger signs. Leave a wide margin around hazards, or walk around them. Reschedule the trip when conditions are simply too dangerous—for instance, during floods or extreme cold. Be conservative! Paddling can be safe, and it should be fun.

Weather

Paddlers must have a basic understanding of weather and weather patterns. To the paddler, weather is a primary concern, and knowledge of some simple weather prediction tools can be invaluable. Weather forecasting, although based on scientific analysis, can be relatively easy to accomplish with some knowhow. Several practical tricks can help you predict the weather with considerable reliability. And all you really have to do is look up to the sky.

For example, the formation of jet vapor trails is a key indicator. The high-altitude air is frequently crisscrossed with trails left by planes. On some days the trails are invisible. On other days they last for a few minutes before vanishing. But at times they seem to last for hours. Some spread slowly and seem to change into clouds. The lingering vapor trail is noteworthy because a trail that remains in the sky usually foretells a change in the weather.

Read the Clouds

An interesting method of weather forecasting is cloud reading. Each type of cloud carries a weather message. From cloud clues you can get a good idea of the type of weather to expect in the next few hours to the next few days (figure 5.1).

The simplest message comes from the perfectly clear day. This sky condition means that the chance of rain or snow is absent. On a partly sunny, partly cloudy day when the sky is filled with loose, fuzzy cumulus clouds, you should watch for any firming up of the clouds. Loose and cottony clouds are harmless. When firm edges start appearing and the clouds take on a definite shape, showers may develop. The faster the clouds develop, the greater the chance that rain will fall. Generally, the weather will take a turn for the worse when small clouds gather and change into larger clouds. A shifting wind and clouds moving in different directions at different heights are also good indications that rain will follow.

Figure 5.1 Reading the clouds will help you predict when bad weather is approaching.

What makes a river so restful to people is that it doesn't have any doubt—it is sure to get where it is going, and it doesn't want to go anywhere else.

Hal Boyle

Watch for Signs

Some signs that fair weather will continue include summer fog clearing before noon, clouds decreasing in number, wind blowing gently from the west or northwest, the sky remaining clear, the sun appearing as a ball of fire, and the moon shining brightly.

Signs that the weather will change for the worse include clouds increasing and lowering, clouds moving in different directions, wind shifting from south to east, clouds darkening the western horizon, the barometer falling, and wind blowing strongly in the early morning.

The weather will clear when the cloud bases increase in height, a cloudy sky begins to clear, the barometer rises rapidly, and wind shifts to a westerly direction.

Obtain Weather Reports

Being able to forecast can be fun and possibly save the day. But you should obtain a reliable weather report before going paddling. Local newspapers often print one- to three-day forecasts. Radio and television broadcasts include weather reports with short- and long-range forecasts. The Internet provides a reliable source of weather information any time of the day.

And, of course, don't forget the special 24-hour weather broadcast by the National Weather Service, a branch of the National Oceanic and Atmospheric Administration (NOAA). Transmitters placed across the country provide the latest weather broadcast directly from the office of the National Weather Service. All you need is a radio with a weather band and you are able to receive regularly updated forecasts for your region. For links to international weather information, visit www.weather.com.

Be Weather Wise

Regardless of how you obtain weather information, heed the warnings. Being weather wise is a basic rule of safe paddling. If you are planning a day on the water, check the local forecast. Remember that you can get into bad weather even with a fair forecast. Squalls and thunderstorms are unpredictable and can cause an enjoyable outing to turn into a dangerous situation. Keep a weather watch, and make the decision to go in to shore if conditions become threatening.

River Reading

Moving water has power. A paddler who understands the principles of moving water can harness this power to have fun on the river. On the other hand, a paddler who doesn't understand and respect these forces can be harmed or even killed by the power of moving water. This section of the chapter covers river dynamics, which provide the foundation for river reading. The dynamics of moving water covered in this section include river currents, river obstacles, and river hazards.

Having an understanding of river dynamics is important for paddlers to ensure an experience that is both safe and enjoyable. Rivers are our drainage systems. Eventually, everything upstream is carried downstream, including natural and human-made debris. The difference between a river feature that can provide endless hours of fun and one that might be dangerous is sometimes subtle. The description of river features and hazards in this chapter can help the paddler have a safe and enjoyable experience.

River Currents

River flows can be complex since gravity, inertia, and obstructions change the way water flows within the banks of any given stream. This section covers many of the ways water reacts to the surrounding environment.

SAFETY TIP

Drifting along in a 5-mile-per-hour (8 kilometer per hour) current may seem tame. But a swamped kayak filled with water can easily exert a force of 2,400 pounds (1,100 kilograms). For this reason you want to be upstream of a swamped kayak so that you do not become caught between a rock and the swamped kayak. Some rivers are measured in cubic feet per second (CFS) or cubic meters per second (CMS), representing the volume of water passing a given point at a given time.

Primary Current

The primary current, the current found in the main channel, refers to the general direction in which the river is flowing. The primary flow is illustrated by a cross section of the river indicating the speed of the flow at various levels (laminar flow). The slowest-moving water is next to the bottom, and each successive layer of water toward the surface flows faster than the layer below it. The fastest-moving water is found just below the surface, because the air next to the surface creates friction that slows the surface water slightly.

A way to conceptualize this principle is to imagine sheets of plywood stacked on the floor with wooden dowels between the sheets (figure 5.2a). Push the stack of plywood. Each sheet of plywood on the stack will travel at the speed of the next lower sheet plus its own speed. Hence, the higher the stack of plywood, the greater the speed that the plywood will travel.

The primary flow can also be illustrated by a top view (figure 5.2b) showing the linear, or surface, flow of the river. As in the laminar flow, the water closest to the river bank is slowest, while the unobstructed center flow is moving fastest.

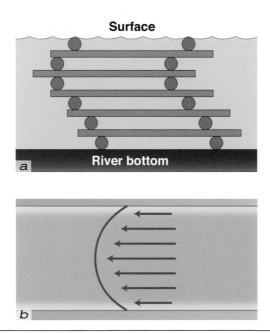

Figure 5.2 Primary current illustrated as (a) laminar flow and (b) surface flow.

Shore-to-Center Flows

Shore-to-center flow refers to the currents moving at the surface of the water from the riverbank to the center channel. Because the water at the surface is traveling slower than the water underneath it, a slight depression is created at the

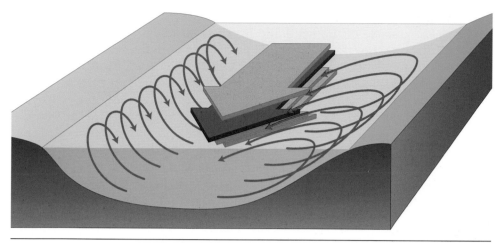

Figure 5.3 Shore-to-center (helical) flow.

surface. To fill the void, water is drawn in from the sides of the river. These flows are sometimes referred to as helical flows (figure 5.3). Because these currents are going away from the shore, a victim who is self-rescuing in higher-volume flow situations may need to swim actively toward the shore to reduce the likelihood of being carried away from shore.

Bends

Rivers tend to meander. When the river bends, inertia forces the main current toward the outside of the bend (figure 5.4). As the deeper, faster, and more powerful current reaches the outside of the bend, it turns downward and creates a spiraling effect off the bottom of the river that leaves more room for surface water on the outside of the bend. The force of the water tends to erode the outside of the bend, causing trees and other debris to fall into the river where they can form strainers.

In contrast, the slower, shallower, and less-powerful current is found on the inside of the bend. A cross section of the current speeds shows the difference between a straight section of river (figure 5.5*a*) and a bend in the river (figure 5.5*b*).

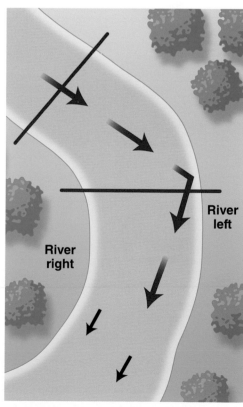

River left

River right

Figure 5.4 Current at a river bend.

Paddlers need to approach bends cautiously. The current can force the kayak to the outside of the bend and into any strainers or obstructions that may be present. Also, if the current is powerful enough, it will tend to push the kayak toward the outside shore of the bend. In addition, the slower water on the inside of the bend can create an effect that can turn the kayak as if it were caught by an eddy. Because the current is going faster toward the outside of the bend, paddlers need to "set" the kayak around the bend to prevent the current from forcing the kayak to the outside of the bend. To set the kayak properly, position it so that the bow is facing the direction of the downstream current just past the inside of the bend (figure 5.6). Once the kayak clears the slower-moving current on the inside of the bend, paddlers can then accelerate forward, avoiding the obstructions and faster current on the outside of the bend.

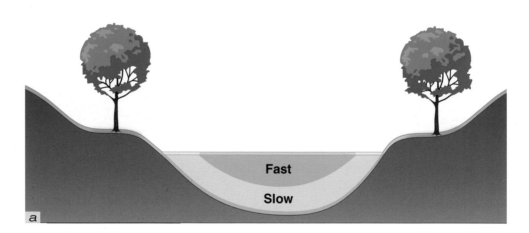

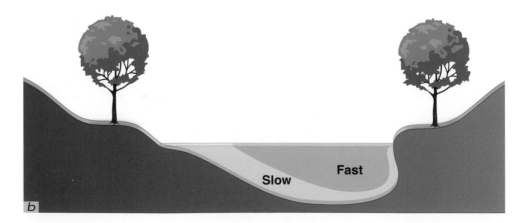

Figure 5.5 Current speed on a *(a)* straight section of the river and a *(b)* bend in the river.

SAFETY TIP

Approach a bend in the river on the inside of the bend where the current is slower and where you can avoid the fast current and any strainers on the outside of the bend.

Chutes and Waves

A constriction forces the water to increase its speed as it passes through it. This usually forms a smooth tongue of water, or a chute (figure 5.7). After the water passes through the constriction, its deceleration into a deeper and slower state results in a series of uniformly spaced, scallop-shaped standing waves. The constriction can vary in width from a boat length to the width of the river. The former can create a drop with small waves that the kayak simply drops through. A riverwide constriction can create large standing waves that can swamp a kayak going through them. On the other hand, these waves often provide ideal waves for surfing the kayak.

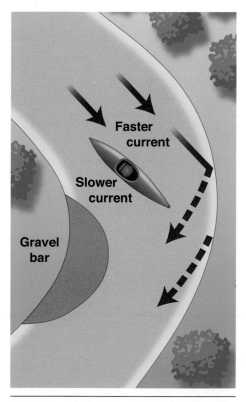

Figure 5.6 To "set" a kayak, point the bow toward the object or bend that you wish to avoid, and back paddle to ferry away from the hazard of danger.

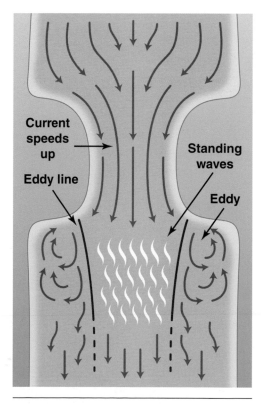

Figure 5.7 Riverwide chute.

Downstream and Upstream Vs

Two rocks or other objects can create a constriction in the water where the water flows between the rocks to form a small chute. The chute of water funnels between the rocks and forms the shape of a V (figure 5.8). The rocks form the two upstream points of the V, and the chute between the rocks forms the downstream point of the V. Often there is a difference in vertical height. Because the water creates a cushion against the rocks, the upstream V will be slightly higher than the chute forming the downstream V, where the water is dropping off. Steer clear of the upstream points, and position the boat to travel down the V for the deepest water.

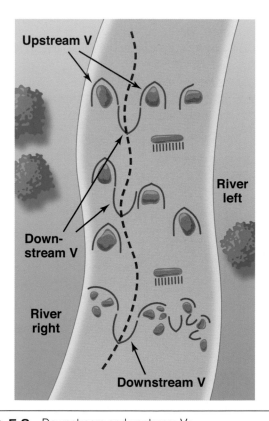

Figure 5.8 Downstream and upstream Vs.

River Obstacles

Rocks are the main obstacles found in rivers. The depth of the rock in the water and its size are key factors in determining its effect on river dynamics. Pillows, holes, and eddies are closely related. A totally submerged rock may have little or no effect on the surface current, while a rock that is closer to the surface will force the water passing over it upward to the surface, creating a small wave, or pillow, downstream from the rock. If the rock is wide, water from the side cannot fill in behind it, creating a depression or void behind the rock. The water flowing over the rock attempts to fill the void, creating a hole, or hydraulic, behind the rock. If the rock is exposed, the water can no longer flow over it and can only fill the void behind the rock from the sides. Eddies are created by the water filling in the void from the sides behind an exposed rock.

Pillows

Water passing over a rock close to the surface is forced upward to the surface, which creates a pillow, a small rounded wave downstream of the rock. The deeper the rock, the farther downstream the pillow is located (figure 5.9*a*). The closer the rock is to the surface, the closer the pillow is to the rock, until the pillow is directly over the rock (figure 5.9*b*). With experience, you will be able to recognize which rocks are close to the surface and need to be avoided and which ones are deep enough not to pose a problem.

A rock that is partway out of the water creates a pillow of water that flows up against it and forms a cushion (figure 5.9*c*). The paddler should avoid the upstream sides of rocks and might have to think and react quickly to keep from being broached (pinned sideways against the underlying rock).

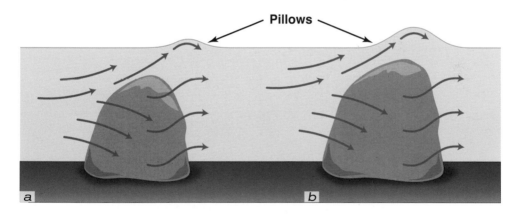

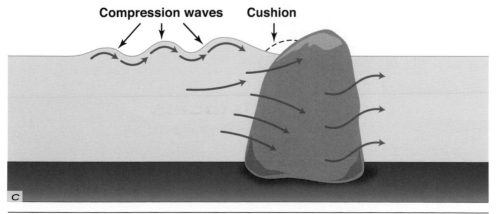

Figure 5.9 Pillows *(a)* downstream of a deep rock, *(b)* over a rock near the surface, and *(c)* upstream of a rock partway out of the water.

Holes

A hole, or hydraulic, occurs in a river where a rock or other obstruction of sufficient width prevents the water from filling the void behind the obstruction from the side, forcing the water to flow over the rock to fill the void or depression. As the water flows over the rock, it plunges down to the bottom of the river and races downstream. As it races downstream, the water shoots back up to the surface, where it moves in one of three directions (figure 5.10). A portion of the water recirculates back upstream to fill the void behind the rock. Farther downstream, some of the water comes up to the surface and continues downstream. This water travels at a slower rate than the general flow of the river and quickly picks up speed as it moves downriver. In between, at the interface of the upstream and downstream flow, the flow is neutral in that it is not really flowing downstream or upstream. This neutral area is called a boil.

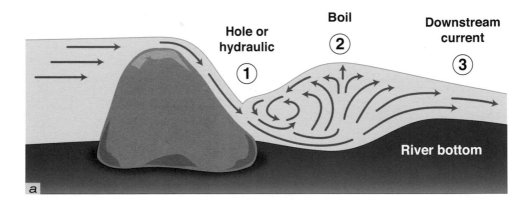

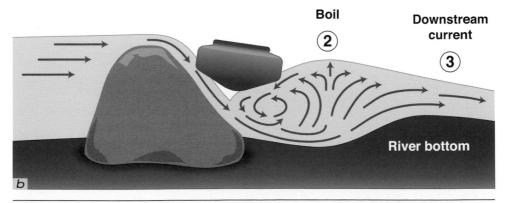

Figure 5.10 *(a)* Hole profile and *(b)* hole profile showing a side surfing kayak.

PADDLER TIP
Love That Rock!

If you find yourself floating sideways toward a rock, lean your body and boat aggressively toward the rock, even putting your hand or paddle on it. The water buffeting off the rock forms a pillow that helps keep your boat off the rock. A round rock tends to be friendlier than one with a sharp, upstream edge. Learn to distinguish between them.

"Love the rock" technique.

The shape of the hole affects how friendly it is to a paddler. If a hole angles downstream it will feed a person and boat out to the downstream end (figure 5.11*a*). If it angles to steep shoreline (figure 5.11*b*), or to another hole, it can be sticky and ugly. If it is straight across the entire river (like a low head dam) it is especially dangerous.

A hole with a few inches or a foot of water going back upstream can be good fun. The dangerous ones have four or five feet of backwash going back upstream. These holes are often called keepers because they keep a kayak or swimmer stuck in them.

If you are paddling a kayak, you can easily feel where you are in the hole. If you are on the upstream side of the boil, you can feel the pull of the current pulling the boat upstream and into the hole. Conversely, if you are on the downstream side of the boil, you can feel the boat slipping downstream and dropping out of the hole.

SAFETY TIP

The differences between holes that are friendly and those that are unfriendly are often subtle. Check with guidebooks and other paddlers before venturing into a questionable hydraulic.

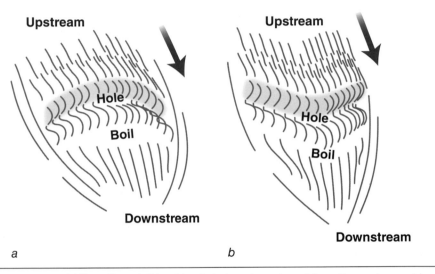

Figure 5.11 *(a)* Friendly and *(b)* unfriendly holes when viewed from the upstream side.

If you are sitting on the shore and watching the kayaker paddle upstream toward the hole in an attempt to surf the wave, you can play a little mental game where you look closely at the attitude of the boat and tell where the kayak is in the hole. Look at the trim of the boat. If the bow is lower than the stern, the kayak is on the wave and will move upstream and into the hole. If the stern is lower than the bow, then the kayak is off the wave and is in the downstream portion. The trim of the kayak is a subtle but good indicator, and watching a kayak in a hole is an enjoyable mental game for the observer. Unless the person paddles hard, he or she is out of the hole and might as well ferry to the shore and try again. Ferrying is a way of moving the boat back and forth in the current without traveling downstream. You will learn more about ferrying in chapter 8.

To evaluate holes, look downstream and beyond to see clues in the current. Is it wavelike, with water splashing up, implying a sloping entry to a fun play hole? Or is it flat, with a horizon line, suggesting that it rushes to a steep drop and pours over into a ledge hole? Watch for water pouring steeply over a rock into a hydraulic and flowing out with the calm look of an eddy. This hole will be less friendly. The amount of water rushing back upstream is a measure of the hole's power.

If you see current downstream, the hole will look more like a wave, indicating deep water. The more a hole resembles a wave, the friendlier it will be. Whitewater dancing up and current or waves just downstream from the hole are friendly characteristics to watch for. If your path takes you into a hole, plan to hit it straight on, perpendicular to the ledge. Reach your strokes over the backwash, and dig into the downstream current. Paddle through it!

Horizon Lines

Occasionally, the water will seem to disappear over the edge of a drop. This horizon line indicates a big drop, one that you will probably want to scout from shore. From a safe place, look for the biggest waves in the main flow of current. Generally, those will direct you to a clear channel and the most fun.

Eddies

Eddies form behind rocks or other obstructions in the river. Water flows past the obstruction, creating a void behind the object that the water attempts to fill. An eddy has three distinct parts (figure 5.12).

The first part of the eddy is where the water in the main current rushes by the rock so fast that water has to flow back upstream to fill the void. This action creates a strong current differential between the main current and the current in the eddy. The interface between the downstream current and the upstream current creates an eddy line or, in extremely fast current, an eddy wall. An eddy wall is created when there is a vertical height difference between the downstream current and the current in the eddy attempting to fill the void behind the rock. If an eddy wall is present, there is a noticeable downhill current inside the eddy. For a paddler, an eddy of this power can be problematic, and the paddler can find the eddy unfriendly. Most eddies, however, have an eddy line with little or no vertical difference between the main current and the upstream current.

The second part of the eddy is the interface between the current moving upstream and the current moving downstream in the eddy. The current here is neutral. In a strong eddy, this

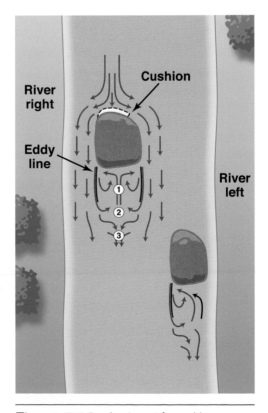

Figure 5.12 Anatomy of an eddy.

PADDLER TIP

When you enter an eddy, look at the shore or some fixed reference point to see whether you are moving upstream or drifting downstream.

is often the ideal location for paddlers to sit. They aren't plastered against the backside of the rock by the upstream current where it is difficult to exit the eddy, and they aren't falling out of the eddy heading downstream either.

The third part of an eddy is where the water in the main current enters the void behind the rock so far downstream that it continues downstream but at a slower rate than the main current. This area of an eddy can be problematic for paddlers because they may think they are in the upstream current in the eddy when they are really moving downstream and quickly falling out of the eddy. In addition, because the current is moving downstream in the eddy, no real eddy line is present in this portion of the eddy. Many beginning paddlers prefer to enter an eddy in this area because no current differential is present and the risk of capsizing is lessened.

Conceptually, the three parts of an eddy have many of the characteristics of a hole. An eddy and a hole are both caused by the river attempting to fill a void. Most eddies are friendly, and paddlers may use them extensively as they travel down a river. In fact, eddy hopping, or traveling deliberately from eddy to eddy, is a good way to move down a challenging section of river.

Remember, however, that some eddies can be violent and unfriendly. Along the edge of the eddy or at the eddy line, water moving in opposite directions creates a current differential. Under normal circumstances, paddlers use the current differential to make an eddy turn. But this same differential can easily capsize a kayak. A strong current differential can create an eddy wall, an actual wall of water between the downstream current and the upstream current in the eddy. These eddies are particularly violent and unfriendly, and they should be avoided. The water is moving in a different direction, and the water moving upstream doesn't move with the same velocity as the downstream flow. This difference in direction and velocity creates a potentially dangerous condition that can spin a kayak around. Depending on the kayak, capsizing is possible, particularly if the paddler is not familiar with what can happen.

Paddlers must consider these differentials in moving water, especially when paddling across them. Speed, power, and crossing angles, in addition to size and type of boat, are important when dealing with the effects of a current differential.

Microcurrents

Microcurrents are currents within other currents. Close examination of the current often reveals that smaller currents may be behaving very differently from the main current around them (figure 5.13).

PADDLER TIP

Recognizing microcurrents is an advanced but important skill. Look at the water and analyze its movement. Look for eddylike currents, slack water, and current differentials behind pillows. These microcurrents can provide refuge for a paddler or, conversely, cause an unwelcome change in the angle of a ferry or other maneuver.

Examination of a chute may reveal a small pillow in it created by a submerged rock. This pillow can be easily overlooked in the water around it. Behind the pillow might be about a boat's length of slack water, which is water that is moving more slowly than the main current surrounding it. A skilled paddler who recognizes this slack water can easily position the boat into the slack water and sit there motionless in the middle of the surrounding fast-moving water.

In a very real sense, the three parts of a hydraulic or the three parts of an eddy constitute microcurrents. For example, a paddler may want no part of a hole. However, close examination of the currents reveal that he can use the slow-moving downstream portion of the hole to perform a ferry to another part of the river.

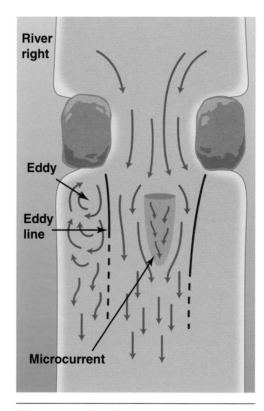

Figure 5.13 Microcurrents.

River Hazards

Rivers present hazards to paddlers for two reasons: Moving water has tremendous power, and rivers can be filled with traps. To appreciate the power of a flowing river, you should understand that water is a heavy element. This weight coupled with movement makes river boating potentially dangerous.

Because water has great weight—1 gallon (3.8 liters) equals 8.3 pounds (3.8 kilograms)—it responds to the physical laws of gravity and inertia. When a river turns, water piles up on the outside of the turn. This bend in the river contributes

SAFETY TIP

If you capsize upstream of a strainer, make every effort to swim away from it. If you are going to be swept into the strainer, turn over on your belly and swim aggressively up and over the strainer. Your life may depend on getting yourself high enough onto the strainer.

to velocity differences. The slow-moving water is found on the inside of the bend. On this inside bend the river deposits silt, and shoaling can occur. If the bend is sharp and narrow, water and debris end up churning about violently, creating an extremely dangerous place.

Obstructions and Strainers

As the river flows, the water meets many obstructions. Bridge abutments and rocks are dangerous simply because they don't move and water does. If the water is moving fast enough, a kayak coming against these types of obstructions can be held fast to their upstream sides. When a kayak is pinned this way, escape is difficult and dangerous. Boat damage is certain, and life can be in serious jeopardy.

Another river danger grows from the presence of obstacles called strainers (figure 5.14). Fallen trees, midstream brush, and collected

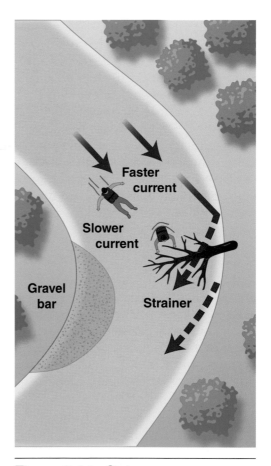

Figure 5.14 Strainer.

debris between rocks and islands can cause serious problems in river traveling. An accumulation of debris may even block an entire river, especially a narrow one. The problem with a strainer is that water flows through these objects while boats and people may not. They can become pinned or trapped against the strainer, making escape difficult and sometimes impossible. Maintaining a good lookout and scouting the river is crucial for avoiding these common obstructions. Strainers are killers! Most commonly formed by trees and rocks, they are extremely dangerous, and paddlers should always avoid them.

SAFETY TIP

Low-head dams are called drowning machines because they are efficient at drowning people. This happens because of the way the water recirculates. There are no natural breaks to allow the water to escape. Look for the horizon line and the abutments. Portage well upstream.

Trees are the most commonly encountered form of strainer found on a river. As the current carves out a bend in a river, it undermines the foundation underneath nearby trees, eventually causing them to fall into the river channel. A strainer on a bend of a river is particularly dangerous because the faster current on the outside of the bend can cause a paddler who is flowing with the current to be swept into the strainer.

Rocks can also cause strainers. Usually, the rocks are positioned on the bottom in such a way that water will flow through them to create a strainer. Often, these strainers are referred to as undercut rocks. Seeing a rock in the current of the river without the typical pillow of water piling up on the upstream side is often a good indication of an undercut rock. Always paddle or swim away from strainers.

High-Water Debris

Spring rain brings flowers, but to the river it brings high-water or flood conditions. High water complicates everything already mentioned. Debris that has collected on the bank of the river floats off. Brush, tree limbs, and sometimes entire trees can be floating down the river. Every spring, paddlers lose their lives on flooded rivers. Paddlers should avoid rivers in flood stage. Another point to ponder is that spring floodwater is cold water!

Low-Head Dams

Low-head dams are designed to create a perfectly formed hydraulic immediately downstream of the dam, diverting most of the energy of the water toward the surface. In addition, this hydraulic extends from one side of the river to the other, right into the dam abutments. A person caught in the recirculating portion of the hydraulic may recirculate endlessly. An unaided person usually drowns.

A horizon line is the usual indicator of a riverwide obstacle such as a waterfall or low-head dam. As you look downriver, you may see a section of calm or smooth-looking water and beyond it a line across the river where the water drops out of sight. Trees on your side of the horizon line will look normal, but trees just downriver from the horizon line often look as if someone cut a section out of their trunks. If a low-head dam forms the horizon line, abutments on each side of the dam usually provide a clear indication of its presence.

SAFETY TIP

Be cautious about paddling and playing behind old human-made structures that might contain reinforcing rods, sharp rocks, and other debris.

Low-head dams have been constructed on rivers both large and small. Most were constructed before people began to use rivers for recreation. The height of the dam is often no more than several feet (a meter or so) above the original channel. Some of the most dangerous low-head dams appear almost level with the water. Low-head dams are potential killers. They are so efficient at this task that they have been called drowning machines.

Waterfalls

Posters and television ads romanticize the adventure of running a waterfall. Running a waterfall, however, is extremely dangerous. Several significant challenges associated with running a waterfall can severely injure you.

- You can land flat in the pool of water below the waterfall and severely compress the disks in your vertebrae.
- The depth of the pool below the waterfall may not be sufficient.
- If you don't have sufficient speed when you go over the falls, your trajectory could take you straight down, where you'll recirculate behind the waterfall. The rock face of the waterfall will be on one side, and the water from the waterfall will be on the other side.

Look for the horizon line and the portage trail so you can carefully and safely portage around waterfalls.

Foot Entrapment

When standing in swift current, your foot can be pushed into a crevice, snarled root, tree limb, or other object. Stand only where the water is knee deep or shallower and the current is slow enough not to be a factor. Shoreline eddies and areas well away from the current may be the best places to stand. Never stand in the main current of a river or stream. Foot entrapments are life threatening. Do not stand up in current.

Old Human-Made Structures

Most rivers contain human-made structures such as old dams or bridge abutments that have fallen into disuse. Sometimes these structures provide a fun place to play with the kayak. Always use caution around these structures.

Life is like swimming in a river. If you don't move upstream, you go backwards.

Unknown

Riprap (rocks, rubble, or other materials used to reinforce shorelines against erosion) may contain large spikes. Old dams and bridge abutments may contain reinforcing rods or sharp rocks that can create nasty injuries. Check the site for hazards at low water. If you have any doubt, find another place to play.

Broaches

A pin, or broach, occurs when a swamped kayak is swept sideways into a rock or other obstruction (figure 5.15). A 5-mile-per-hour (8 kilometer per hour) current can exert more than a ton of pressure (2,400 pounds, or 1,100 kilograms) on a kayak full of water. When that kayak becomes pinned on a rock, the force of the water can easily wrap the boat around the rock. In any potential pinning situation, the paddler should stay on the upstream side of the kayak. If you are swimming with the kayak, try to keep the kayak parallel to the current. If there is any question, leave the kayak and rescue yourself.

Although a kayak can easily broach and become trapped in a strainer, rocks are more commonly responsible for pinning a kayak on a river. The most common pin is the midship pin, or center pin, in which the rock meets the center of the kayak (figure 5.15*a*). If you can influence the pin in any way, try to have the pin occur off the center of the kayak so that extricating it from the rock is easier.

SAFETY TIP

Always swim upstream of the kayak, and attempt to keep the kayak parallel to the main current. If there is any question, let the kayak go and rescue yourself.

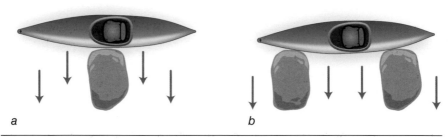

a   b

Figure 5.15   *(a)* Center pin and *(b)* double-end pin.

A double-end, or end-to-end, pin is a particularly nasty situation in which the two ends of the kayak are each caught on a rock and the current pushes the center of the kayak downstream between the rocks (figure 5.15*b*).

Drowning-Trap Flows

A river can be hazardous at any water level. Ask knowledgeable people about flow rates to determine the best times and conditions to paddle sections of the river, and avoid situations that are particularly dangerous. Most people associate danger with floodlike conditions such as muddy water, water flowing over the banks, water in the trees, floating debris, and big waves. Floods and high water are dangerous, and most people recognize the danger and stay off the river.

However, on many rivers, recreational fatalities tend to occur at moderate water levels, when the river is well within its banks and looks perfectly normal. The normal cycle of flows for rivers is that during the summer, when most people visit, the water level drops to the point where moving water is less of a contributing factor in such fatalities. However, as the water level rises, risks increase, and in some cases the river becomes extremely dangerous.

Three components define a drowning-trap flow: depth, velocity, and deceptiveness. At moderate flows the river has the power (depth and velocity) to drown, yet it is deceptive because people tend to associate danger with flood conditions rather than with moderate flows. The cross-sectional profile of a typical eastern river illustrates the relationship between moderate drowning-trap flows, summer low flows, and flood levels that people normally perceive as being dangerous (figure 5.16).

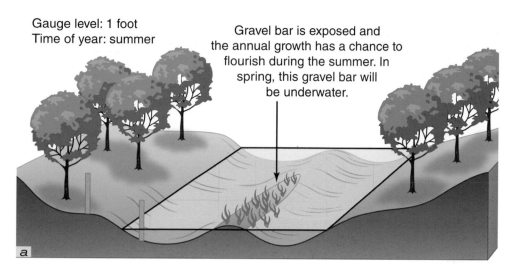

Gauge level: 1 foot
Time of year: summer

Gravel bar is exposed and the annual growth has a chance to flourish during the summer. In spring, this gravel bar will be underwater.

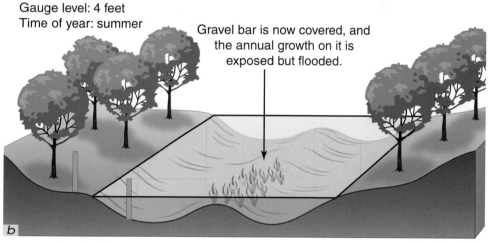

Gauge level: 4 feet
Time of year: summer

Gravel bar is now covered, and the annual growth on it is exposed but flooded.

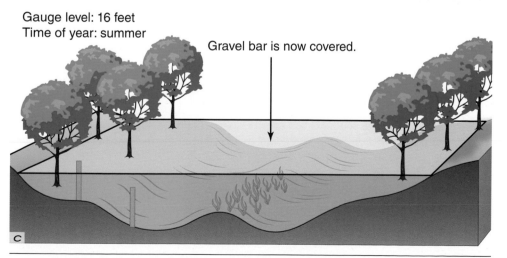

Gauge level: 16 feet
Time of year: summer

Gravel bar is now covered.

Figure 5.16 *(a)* Drowning-trap flow with 1-foot (.3 meter) gauge, *(b)* drowning-trap flow with 4-foot (1.2 meter) gauge, and *(c)* flood with 16-foot (5 meter) gauge.

SAFETY TIP

Moderate water levels are dangerous because people don't recognize the danger of the moving water. For example, a person standing thigh deep in a 5-mile-per-hour (8 kilometer per hour) current can easily have 100 pounds (45 kilograms) of pressure placed on his or her body. This amount of pressure is often enough to upend the person. Even experts have difficulty determining water levels, so look for telltale signs along the river, particularly annual vegetation on gravel bars that is partially underwater.

The depth of the water is a key determinant of its velocity and power. Imagine standing in moving water about waist deep. With some deliberate care, you can brace yourself against the current and stand in the water. Add another foot of water so that the water is above your waist. Now the river current can easily move you. It may knock you off your feet and sweep you downstream. When the speed of the current reaches that of a person walking fast, it begins to have the power to move you, knock you over, and, depending on circumstances, drown you.

Annual vegetation that invades the gravel bars and other areas of the river during early summer is a good, practical indicator of drowning-trap water levels. Look for areas that were underwater during spring runoff. When vegetation in these places becomes either partially or fully underwater, the river is higher than normal and may be in the drowning-trap flows.

The last component of the drowning-trap flow is deceptiveness. A river well within its banks looks perfectly normal to the casual visitor. However, if that visitor's frame of reference is a once-a-year trip, what is perceived as normal may actually be high water. A river that is not flooding and looks normal may have the depth and velocity to contribute to an accident.

Capsizing

Most paddlers have a story to tell about unexpectedly ending up in the water. Most will laugh and chuckle at the memory of the clumsy mishap. Some may portray it as a narrow escape. A fact of life in paddlesports is that if you spend much time at all on the water, you will eventually take an unexpected plunge. Most of the time, the event is no big deal, especially if you are a swimmer and are wearing a properly fitted life jacket (turn to chapter 3). But if the water is

SAFETY TIP

The number one thing you can do to stay safe on the water is to always wear a life jacket (personal flotation device, or PFD). Accidents happen fast, even to the most experienced paddlers. Having a life jacket stowed in the kayak is not enough. Drowning remains the leading cause of death in recreational kayaking accidents. Why risk it? Always wear your life jacket. For information regarding proper fit and care of your PFD, turn to chapter 3.

cold and no one is available to assist, a fall overboard can be a risky event, so keeping a kayak from capsizing becomes essential.

Understanding boat stability is an important skill in using a kayak. Boat stability is related directly to the below-water hull shape and the height of the center of gravity. The lower and closer the load in the boat is placed to the center line of the boat, the more stable the boat will be, assuming that adequate freeboard remains. If this load is moved off-center, forces created by buoyancy respond to the boat hull to balance the boat. The forces of gravity and buoyancy are equal when the boat is at rest.

The real problem develops when weight is added above the deck of the boat, which raises the center of gravity in the boat. The center of gravity is the point where the total weight of the craft and everything aboard could hypothetically be centered in one spot and produce the same effect on the hull. In a kayak the weight above the deck is people—people moving around, people paddling and reaching too far, people doing everything that people do! If this elevated center of gravity is off-center, such as when a person leans over the side of the boat, the force of buoyancy may not be able to counterbalance the change in the location of the center of gravity, resulting in either a swamp or a capsize. In a lightweight kayak, the forces trying to right the boat may kick the craft right out from under the paddler, resulting in a fall overboard and a capsize.

To prevent an unexpected plunge into the water, do the following:

- **Maintain body weight over the center line.** In other words, keep your nose over your navel.

- **Maintain three points of contact while moving around in a kayak.** Like a stable three-legged stool, a person keeping three points of contact retains stability (see figure 5.17). If you move a foot to step forward, you should be holding on to the boat with both hands.

Figure 5.17   Maintain three points of contact for balance.

- **Load the boat properly.** Keep the weight centered from both side to side and bow to stern. And you don't want a lot of stuff in your kayak, even on a camping trip. Never overload the craft.
- **Practice proper retrieval.** When retrieving something from the water, use a paddle or move the boat close to the object so that you can grab the item from the water without leaning your shoulders over the side of the boat.

These techniques take practice, but they will soon become instinctive and protect you from going overboard.

Of course, wind, current, and waves affect the stability of the most carefully loaded and paddled kayak. A wake from a powerboat can surprise even attentive paddlers. If you are not a swimmer, take the time to learn how to swim. Capsizing a kayak is part of the sport. Swimmer or not, always wear your life jacket.

Cold-Water Safety and Survival Skills

Paying attention to cold water is a practical thing. You will not have fun if you are cold, so it is best to understand the effect of cold water and appropriately deal with it.

Some of the best paddling opportunities occur in spring and fall when cooler weather and cold water increase the risks associated with getting wet. All paddlers should take the precautions necessary to be able to enjoy safe kayaking under these conditions. Carefully read and adhere to the advice to increase your odds of survival should you capsize or encounter bad weather.

Avoid Cold-Water Shock and Hypothermia

You should try to avoid two things: cold-water shock and hypothermia. Cold-water shock is a dangerous, sometimes fatal, condition that can result when a person is suddenly immersed in cold water, such as would occur in a capsize. The sudden exposure of the head and chest to cold water typically causes an involuntary gasp for air, a sudden increase in heart rate and blood pressure, and disorientation and can possibly cause cardiac arrest. The only remedy for cold-water shock is to be properly dressed for a plunge and to get the individual out of the water. You should then keep an eye out for symptoms of hypothermia.

Hypothermia is a dangerous and sometimes fatal condition that results when exposure to cold prevents the body from maintaining its normal temperature in the core region (heart, lungs, and the rest of the torso). Although this condition can occur through exposure to cold air alone, its onset occurs much more quickly when the body is wet or immersed in water. Paddlers must take special care to protect themselves from this danger when they paddle in cold water, rainy conditions, or cool air temperatures.

The most typical symptoms of hypothermia usually appear in this general order:

1. Shivering
2. Impaired judgment
3. Clumsiness
4. Loss of manual dexterity
5. Slurred speech
6. Inward behavior, withdrawal
7. Cessation of shivering
8. Muscle rigidity
9. Unconsciousness

The method of treatment depends on the severity of the hypothermia. One basic thing to remember is that the individual must be warmed slowly.

- **Mild hypothermia** (victim shivering but coherent): Move the victim to a place of warmth. Replace wet clothes with dry ones from your equipment bag. Give warm, sweet drinks, but no alcohol or caffeine. Keep the victim warm for several hours.

- **Moderate hypothermia** (shivering may decrease or stop): The victim may seem irrational, with deteriorating coordination. Use the same treatment as for mild hypothermia but offer no drinks. Keep the victim lying down with the torso, thighs, head, and neck covered with dry clothes, coats, or blankets to stop further heat loss. Seek medical attention immediately.

- **Severe hypothermia** (shivering may have stopped): The victim may resist help or be semiconscious or unconscious. After being removed from water, the victim must be kept prone, on his back, and immobile. The victim must be

(continued on page 108)

COMMUNICATION

While you are on the water, there may be times when you will not be able to speak or even shout instructions to others in your group. For that reason, it is important that paddlers be able to communicate with others using universal paddle and whistle signals. When given a signal on the water, respond with the same signal to acknowledge your understanding and confirm the signal.

- **Stop**—Hold the paddle horizontally overhead. All paddlers should stop in a safe location and look at the person signaling for more information (photo *a*).
- **Help or emergency**—Wave the paddle from side to side or give three or more long blasts on a whistle. All paddlers should look at the person signaling for more information. Only those trained in rescue for emergency response should directly assist. Other paddlers should remain at a safe distance or in a safe location. In some cases, they may be asked to go for help (photos *b-c*).

a

b

c

- **All clear**—Hold the paddle vertically and stationary. Paddlers may return to normal paddling protocols (photo *d*).

- **Go this way**—Use the paddle to point toward the direction of travel. Point to the clear way, not to the hazard or obstruction. Paddlers responding to the signal should go in the direction indicated (photo *e*).

- **Are you OK?**—Tap the top of your head three times and point to the person whom you are questioning. If the person taps his or her head three times in response, the person is OK. Otherwise, assistance is needed (photo *f*).

(continued from page 105)

handled gently. Cover the torso, thighs, head, and neck with dry covers to stop further heat loss. Do not stimulate the arms and legs in any manner because cold blood in the extremities that suddenly returns to the core may induce cardiac arrest. Seek medical attention immediately.

Reduce Your Exposure

To reduce your exposure to cold water, take the following precautions:

- Dress in layers using synthetic fabrics such as polyester fleece to prevent becoming overheated or chilled from perspiration. Avoid wearing cotton when paddling in cool or cold weather.
- Carry a waterproof jacket designed for splash and rain protection. When the water temperature is less than 60 degrees Fahrenheit (16 degrees Celsius), wear specialized insulating clothing capable of protecting you while in the water.
- You should always wear a wet suit or dry suit if
  1. the combined air and water temperature is below 120 degrees Fahrenheit (49 degrees Celsius),
  2. the water temperature is below 60 degrees Fahrenheit (16 degrees Celsius),
  3. you will be far from shore on cold water, or
  4. you expect to be repeatedly exposed to cold water in cool or mild weather. Keep in mind that the best type of wet suit for paddling is the Farmer John style and that the warmth and comfort range of a dry suit will vary based on the clothing worn underneath it.
- Wear a warm hat that will stay on your head in the water. A fleece-lined skullcap is ideal.

SAFETY TIP

All paddlers need to be prepared for these circumstances:

- Low light conditions
- The need to contact help
- Minor medical emergencies
- Outings that extend past the estimated return time
- Weather pattern changes
- Other boat traffic

SAFETY TIP

Any decision to swim for the shore of a lake should not be made lightly. Physical activity such as swimming or other struggling in the water increases heat loss. Survival time can fall to minutes. Strong swimmers have died before they could swim 100 yards (90 meters) in cold water. In water colder than 40 degrees Fahrenheit (4 degrees Celsius), victims have experienced "swim failure" and have drowned before they could swim 100 feet (30 meters). Also keep in mind that judging distance accurately on the water is difficult.

- Have spare dry clothing stored in a sealed dry bag while on the water. If you become wet, change into dry clothing at the first sign of shivering.
- Test your protective clothing in a controlled cold-water environment to understand the level of protection provided.
- Know the water temperature before you set out. Recognize that dam-released water can be significantly colder than expected.
- Always wear your life jacket (PFD).
- Paddle near shore or near others who can help you in the event of a capsize.
- Keep your body well fueled with high-carbohydrate foods and plenty of water.

Know What to Do if You Capsize

In the event of a capsize in cold water, follow these steps:

- Get out of the water, and dry off as quickly as possible.
- After you are out of the water, put on dry clothes if you are not already wearing appropriate cold protective gear.
- If you are unable to exit the water quickly, keep calm, remain with your boat, conserve energy, and get in the HELP (heat escape lessening posture) position: Fold your arms against your chest, cross your legs, and keep still until help arrives (see figure 5.18).
- If two or more people are in the water, get into the huddle posture: Put your arms around one another, stay close together, and keep still (see figure 5.19).
- Attempt to swim to shore only if
    - the chance of rescue is small or nil,
    - you are in danger of floating into dangerous rapids or other hazards, or
    - you are certain that you can make it.

Figure 5.18   HELP posture.

Figure 5.19   Huddle posture.

Summary

Good paddling is about boat control. Mastering control on a lake or river requires thorough knowledge of the various forces involved. Learning to read the weather, rivers, and water enables you to apply the proper strokes and maneuvers to adjust your speed and assess the situation. These essential skills should keep you out of harm's way.

Bear in mind, however, that this text is designed to be used by recreational kayakers as a supplementary resource. It is not intended to replace on-water instruction by a qualified instructor.

Group Safety

Prepare your boat and equipment for the activity according to the following list:

☐ Make sure your life jacket fits and that you wear it properly adjusted.

☐ Your boat must have flotation sufficient to float it when swamped.

☐ Inspect your boat and repair any damage before launch.

☐ Install and inspect end lines so that the boat is easy to hold on to when you are in the water.

☐ Inspect your paddles and safety gear such as pumps or bailers, navigational aids, and rescue gear before each trip.

☐ Carry a more-than-adequate supply of food, drinking water, and protective clothing in waterproof containers.

☐ Ideally, every trip should have among its participants several persons certified in CPR (cardiopulmonary resuscitation); first aid or wilderness first response; and boat rescue, capsize, and recovery. Bring a suitable first aid kit and an emergency repair kit, and know how to use them.

Prepare as a group and know the responsibilities of group members.

☐ Research the trip. Know the distance, likely conditions, potential hazards, and bail-out points so that you are prepared should conditions worsen.

☐ Know each participant's abilities and goals. Pick an activity level that matches the ability of the group.

☐ The participant with the least experience, skill, and ability must be able to complete the trip safely.

☐ All participants should accept responsibility for their own safety and be ready, willing, and able to assist others in the group as appropriate to their level of training and knowledge.

☐ Identify a trip planner to arrange meeting locations and shuttles, identify equipment needs, and file a float plan for the group. The group must have the knowledge, skills, and equipment to deal with potential hazards.

☐ Do a group briefing, including an equipment check, at the put-in.

☐ Start as a cohesive group, stay together while under way, and take out as a group. The group's mutual protection promotes individual safety.

☐ See and be seen. Keep a safe distance from other boats. Maintain a route that avoids other boats. Avoid hazards.

Capsizing

- ☐ If you realize you are about to capsize, hold your breath to minimize gasping when entering the water.

- ☐ Check yourself for injuries, and get control of your emotions.

- ☐ If paddling tandem, check to see whether your partner is OK. If your partner needs assistance, provide what is needed and possible.

- ☐ Focus on staying calm and helping your partner stay calm.

- ☐ Retrieve paddles, the boat, and any other loose equipment.

- ☐ Stay with the boat while deciding which rescue technique (see chapter 6) to use.

PART II

On the Water

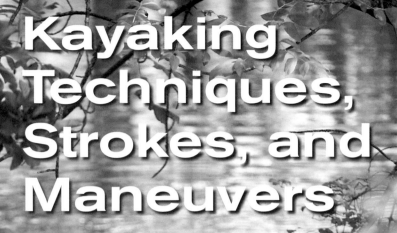

CHAPTER 6

Kayaking Techniques, Strokes, and Maneuvers

Energy is the essence of life. Every day you decide how you're going to use it by knowing what you want and what it takes to reach that goal, and by maintaining focus.

Oprah Winfrey

Now that you are properly equipped and understand the risks involved in the sport, you are ready to master the basic skills of kayaking. The objective of paddling is to make the kayak go where you want it to go with efficiency and safety. You use strokes to accomplish that goal. Some strokes make the kayak respond better than other strokes (efficiency) without risk of shoulder dislocation or injury (safety).

In this chapter, you will learn how to get the boat to the water and enter it in a balanced manner. You will also learn fundamentals of boat control and movement and the strokes that form the basis of most kayak paddling techniques. You will then learn how to combine these strokes to form new strokes and how to modify them in infinite combinations to make the kayak go where you want it to go. Finally, you will learn key safety and rescue skills that are essential for both you and your fellow paddlers when out on the water.

The structure of this chapter uses three distinct and useful levels of skill development: basic strokes, compound strokes, and customized strokes. Basic strokes are important because they form the foundation of most of the other strokes you will perform. Strokes are presented here in their pure form. In reality, most paddling is a hybrid of strokes that allows the paddler to reach the ultimate goal of proper boat placement.

Getting Ready

Whether you'll do most of your kayaking on whitewater, in tidal water, or on flatwater, you need to learn a few skills before taking that first kayaking outing. Practice the skills in this section on some calm water until you've mastered them. Then you'll be well prepared for whitewater or the open sea.

PADDLING SAFETY TIPS

Paddling

- Paddling in groups of three or more is generally safer.
- Do not use drugs or alcohol while on the water.
- Boat politely—look out for yourself and everyone else on the water.
- Boat conservatively—stay within your skill level.
- Hands-on instruction makes paddling safer and more fun.

Other Activities

- Anglers and hunters should be extra vigilant about weight shifts, appropriate equipment, and life jacket use.
- Dogs should wear properly fitted life jackets.
- Anticipate sudden movements from dogs in boats.

Carrying the Boat

You'll see the most experienced paddlers carrying their boats on their shoulders to get down to the water. But there's no reason you shouldn't start by pairing off with someone to tandem carry the boat. The grab loops at the boat's bow and stern work well as handles to hold while carrying a boat. Lift with your legs rather than your back to avoid straining your lower back. If you're carrying on your own, take time to figure out how to use your legs to bounce the boat up on your shoulder and how to use your foot to snag the paddle and bring it up into your other hand. Sea kayaks are very awkward to carry solo, so nearly everyone pairs up or uses specially designed carts.

One-Person Carry

A single person executes a solo carry (figure 6.1). The person carries the kayak over the shoulder by resting one side of the cockpit on the shoulder, balancing the kayak with the opposite hand. Since kayaks can weigh up to 60 to 70 pounds (27 to 32 kilograms), this is a challenging carry for long distances but can be advantageous on winding and tight portage trails.

Figure 6.1   One-person kayak carry.

SAFETY TIP

Be especially careful of lifting your boat when you are cold and wet or when the boat is full of water.

Two-Person Carry

In this carry (figure 6.2), two people carry the kayak to make it less strenuous. They begin by standing on opposite sides of the boat, one at the bow and the other at the stern. Each grabs a toggle or carry handle in one hand, and they carry the boat at about thigh level as if carrying a suitcase. Four people, one at each end and two per side, using the cockpit combing, can carry heavier loads.

Getting Into the Boat

Getting into the kayak on the water without a flip can be tricky. A sandy beach is an ideal place to put in for the first time. Simply sit on the back deck of the kayak while it is still on land with the front (bow) of the kayak in the water, slide your legs into the cockpit and sit in the kayak, which should be pointed toward the water, and scoot your way into the water.

Figure 6.2 Two-person carry.

A rocky shoreline, a dock, and an expensive boat force you to put the boat in the water, parallel to shore, and use the paddle for stability while getting in (figure 6.3). Put the paddle behind your cockpit, with one blade up on shore—powerface up. Sit on the ground or dock in front of the paddle shaft, with your back to it, and reach directly behind you to grab it. Load most of your weight on the part of the paddle that's on the boat, but keep a little bit of weight on the part of the paddle closer to the shore. While bracing yourself on shore, position yourself on the back deck of the kayak, and slide both legs at the same time into the boat until your butt rests on the seat.

Putting the Spray Skirt On

Not all kayaks use spray skirts. If you do use one, getting the spray skirt, especially a new one, onto the cockpit rim can also be tricky. With your skirt already pulled high on your waist, begin from a sitting position, and lean back to pull the skirt to your waist or slightly above it (figure 6.4). Then reach behind and hook the back of the spray skirt to the rim. Drag your elbows forward and across the skirt, positioning the sides. Reach forward to hook the front of the skirt to the cockpit rim. Adjust the sides last. This step can be frustrating, but don't be afraid to ask for help. It's simply an awkward maneuver that sometimes requires a little assistance. If you are going to use a spray skirt, be sure that you get proper instruction on how to release it both on land and in the water.

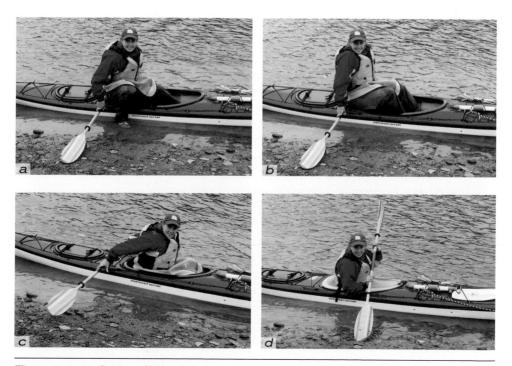

Figure 6.3 Getting into the kayak.

Figure 6.4 Putting the spray skirt on.

Capsizing

Capsizing is part of the sport of kayaking. Paddlers must always be prepared to swim by dressing properly and wearing a life jacket. Once in the water, hang on to your boat and paddle if possible. Wind and waves can easily separate you from your boat. Remain calm and breathe.

To get back on a sit-on-top boat, use the BBL (belly-butt-legs) technique to reenter the boat. First flip the boat upright. Pull your belly on your boat, then your butt, then your legs in the boat. The self-bailing hull allows any water to drain away from the cockpit area. This makes these boats ideal in warm surf. Be sure to practice in calm water before paddling in more-challenging conditions.

If you flip in a kayak with a cockpit, put your hands on the boat next to your hips and push out of the boat. With a spray skirt, you'll need to take a few extra seconds to pull the grab loop to release the skirt from the boat before you push out.

Rescues are discussed in more detail later in this chapter. As you progress in the sport, you might enjoy learning more-advanced techniques, such as the paddle float rescue or even the kayak roll.

Wet Exit

Early in your first day of kayaking, you should learn and practice a wet exit (figure 6.5). This is simply the process of swimming out of the boat after it flips upside down. You should be underwater for about 5 to 10 seconds maximum. Being relaxed in a kayak demands that you be comfortable hanging out underwater. Practice the wet exit until you can do it in a slow, controlled manner. Use of nose plugs is optional but can make a difference in your ability to concentrate, so they are highly recommended when learning this technique.

Here are the steps for a wet exit:

- Take a deep breath.
- Tuck forward for protection and to orient yourself.
- Flip over.
- While upside down, practice tapping your hands on the bottom of the boat three times to relax and remain oriented.
- Grab the grab-loop, push away and pull up to release the spray skirt from the kayak.
- Put your hands on either side of your hips, adjacent to the cockpit rim.
- Push out of the boat like taking off a pair of pants.
- Push back farther, until your legs are free of the cockpit and your life jacket can float you to the surface.
- When you get to the surface, hold the kayak with one hand and the paddle with the other. Try to maintain contact with your boat for safety and visibility.

After your first few wet exits, get a friend to help you empty your boat. Then, with a little practice, you can try placing one end on shore and lifting the other end to drain water. Lift with your legs to avoid back injury!

Figure 6.5 Practicing a wet exit.

TECHNIQUE TIP

Remain tucked forward when doing a wet exit. A common problem is leaning back and trying to swim to the surface. This actually tangles your legs and makes the wet exit feel more difficult and rushed than necessary.

Balancing Skills

Start from a comfortable position in the boat. Your feet should be resting comfortably on foot pedals. Many cockpit boats have knee or thigh braces, which should be adjusted to fit you comfortably. Above all, you should feel comfortable in the boat and should feel able to move the boat with leg, feet, and hip movements.

Before working on specific strokes and maneuvers, start by making sure your position in the boat is relaxed and balanced. Sit comfortably with your chest forward and chin up.

Balance is obviously an important part of kayaking. If your whole body is stiff, you'll flip. To balance easily and use a wide variety of strokes, you'll need to be flexible. Gently stretch your muscles before and after you paddle (see chapter 2 for some suggested stretches for improving flexibility for paddling). Good posture will allow a full torso twist needed for basic kayak strokes. This section discusses ways to lean and edge the boat to help you develop good balance.

Leans, and the resulting good balance, are an important part of learning to paddle, but they are rarely described with precision. Leans can be categorized into three types: the bell buoy lean, the body lean, and the J-lean (see figure 6.6).

Bell Buoy Lean

The bell buoy lean is named for the stiff rocking action of an ocean bell buoy. Navigation bell buoys are so bottom heavy that they are self-righting. Boats aren't that way, so bell buoy leans in a kayak require support from the paddle. This makes it an inappropriate whitewater lean.

Practice the bell buoy lean by sitting straight up. While maintaining a straight back, shift the weight to one hip, allowing your upper body to tilt to the same side. If you do not correct your posture, you will eventually capsize the boat, resulting in a need to wet exit, perform a self-rescue, or be rescued.

Body Lean

The body lean leaves the boat flat while the body leans. Beginners like this lean since the boat feels securely flat. Unfortunately, a flat boat usually defeats the purpose of the lean. Beginning paddlers are easily fooled into thinking they are leaning the boat when in fact they are just leaning their bodies. This lean is intuitive for most, and time must be spent to "unlearn" this type of lean.

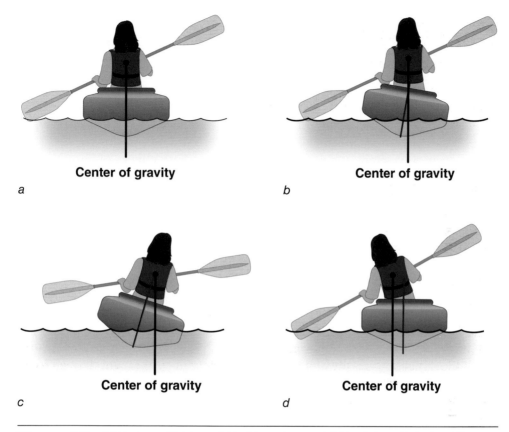

Figure 6.6 *(a)* No lean, *(b)* J-lean, *(c)* bell buoy lean, and *(d)* body lean. Note the difference in center of gravity and boat tilt in each of these leans.

SAFETY TIP
Boat Stability

- Keep your shoulders inside the width of the boat.
- Load the boat evenly from bow to stern and left to right.
- Keep your nose over your belly button for best stability.
- Keep weight low, and balance left to right for best stability.
- Boat design plays a big role in stability. Practice balance techniques under the guidance of a credentialed kayak instructor to discover primary and secondary stability traits of your boat.

J-Lean

The best lean to use is the J-lean. The J-lean, named for the shape of your spine when the lean is done correctly, is a boat lean with your body weight centered over the boat. This lean keeps most of the weight off your blade so you can use it for balance and for strokes.

Learning and practicing the J-lean is best done on flatwater. First lean your boat, and feel how the weight and pressure change from both knees and hips to just one. Thrust out your ribs, and physically lift the opposite knee.

Feel how the weight and pressure change from both cheeks of your bottom to just one. Keep your body comfortably relaxed over the boat, with your head centered over its center. Rock the boat over to edge on the other side, and try the same maneuver. This will give you a good feel for the boat's stability. Master kayakers don't rely on their paddles for support, even with their boats on edge, using the J-lean to provide balance.

Notice how a good J-lean requires that your head be cocked away from the direction of the lean, allowing for more body flexibility. If you can hold that lean for a while, try paddling forward while you maintain a slight J-lean. Transferring this drill to rougher water will be even better for developing your balance. If these drills are difficult, you might practice the torso stretches discussed in chapter 2.

Concepts of Paddling

Paddling is the art and science of moving a kayak through the water. The key is to maximize body and paddle efficiency in order to move your boat. For best effect, keep the paddle blade at right angles to the direction of travel; efficiency fades quickly as the angle changes. Keep the shaft vertical to the water surface when moving forward or in reverse. Keep the shaft horizontal on sweep strokes, which are used to turn the boat. Focus on moving the boat toward your paddle. These concepts of paddling describe fundamental information that applies to all paddling disciplines: whitewater, flatwater, and river.

Boat Moves to the Paddle

The objective of paddling is to move the boat through the water. The paddle is the lever. In a very real sense, the paddler is levering the kayak through the water. It is easy to lose sight of this fundamental principle when describing strokes and when diagramming the stroke moving through the water. Here are two things to remember:

1. Hold the paddle horizontally for turning strokes and vertically for power strokes.
2. Use your torso muscles. The arms should be viewed as "struts" to connect the paddle to the torso. The real power generates from the torso.

The following definitions are provided to assist your learning in this chapter.

- Power face of the blade—When performing the forward stroke, the power face is the side of the blade that is moving through the water. It is facing the stern, or back, of the kayak.
- Working blade—The blade in the water when performing any stroke.
- Back face of the blade—When performing the forward stroke, the back face of the blade is the other side of the blade. It is facing the bow or front of the kayak (see figure 3.7 in chapter 3).
- Basic strokes—The power phase of the stroke forms a uniform motion through the water. The blade is perpendicular to the axis of travel.
- Compound strokes—Two or more basic strokes are combined to make a compound stroke. Compound strokes can easily be broken down into their basic strokes.
- Customized strokes—Customized strokes are derived from basic or compound strokes. However, the blade of the paddle moves through the water at an angle that is not perpendicular to the stroke. For example, the stationary draw is a customized stroke because the blade requires the forward motion of the kayak.

Types of Strokes

Generally, there are three types of strokes: dynamic, stationary, and bracing strokes.

- Dynamic strokes are strokes that move in relationship to the position of the paddler. Most strokes are dynamic. They include the forward, reverse, and draw as well as most other strokes.
- Stationary strokes (static strokes) are strokes where the paddle is held in a fixed position relative to the paddler. Stationary strokes require the movement of the kayak through the water or the river current to make the stroke work effectively. The stationary draw is an example of a stationary stroke.
- Bracing strokes are primarily used to stabilize the kayak. In the right circumstances, a stationary draw can be used as a bracing stroke.

Parts of a Stroke

Dynamic strokes have three phases: the catch, propulsion and recovery. The catch or plant refers to the entry of the paddle at the beginning of the propulsion phase. The propulsion phase is that part of the stroke that moves the kayak through the water. The recovery phase is the portion of the stroke that returns the blade to the catch or plant position. The recovery phase can occur either in or out of the water. Since stationary strokes are held stationary in the water, they have propulsion but not a recovery phase. When discussing the individual strokes in this chapter, the description includes both the propulsion and recovery phases of the stroke. Where applicable, the catch is also discussed.

Figure 6.7 A grip and control hand.

Holding the Paddle

Most, but not all, kayak paddle blades are offset: When you lay the paddle on the ground, the blades face in different directions. This offset, or blade feathering, makes the paddle easier to use in a head wind and allows for more power on a wide variety of strokes.

The offset blades affect how you grip the paddle shaft. One hand, the control hand, remains indexed (i.e., it stays in the same place on the shaft) (figure 6.7). Ninety-five percent of paddles in the United States are right-hand controlled, which makes your right hand the control hand. Some people prefer left-controlled paddles. However, there's little evidence that a left-controlled paddle will ease your learning, regardless of which hand is dominant for you.

Many recreational and sea kayakers switch the offset, or feathering, of their paddles to alleviate arm strain, and paddling with nonfeathered paddles is also common. But we assume that you are using the more common offset paddle. Your control hand holds the shaft, with the top of your knuckles lined up with the upper edge of the blade. The opposite hand has a relaxed grip so the paddle can rotate in that hand.

PADDLER TIP

A common paddling error is holding the shaft with a two-hand death grip. This is tiring and ineffective. Remember to relax the non–control hand during every stroke. Let the paddle shaft rotate freely between strokes.

Taking Your First Stroke

Every stroke includes both a push with one arm and a pull with the other. Your control hand holds the shaft, with the top of your knuckles lined up with the top of the blade. This orientation ensures that during a stroke on the right side of the kayak, your right forearm continues pulling in the desired direction. Your left arm is pushing the stroke through. A stroke on the left-side begins with cocking your control-hand wrist up (like revving a motorbike). This movement turns the left-side blade in the position of a forward stroke. During the pull of this stroke, you'll be gripping with your left hand while your right hand pushes. Rotate the paddle shaft back into position for a stroke on the right by relaxing the left hand. Keeping the fingers extended on the top pushing arm allows a fluid movement.

Perform all strokes with your arms stationed comfortably in front of your body at a level between your belly button or chest, depending on the power needed for the stroke. This position prevents your arms from becoming over-extended or in an awkward place. During strokes that sweep to the boat's end, you will turn your torso to maintain your arms in the proper position.

Holding the paddle correctly will increase your stroke power and decrease your chances of tendinitis. Keep your control hand fixed on the shaft, ready for an optimal pull. Allow the shaft to rotate in the other hand. Avoid holding on too tightly by relaxing your top hand during each stroke.

Stroke Techniques

Knowing how to balance and edge the boat while sitting up straight and holding the paddle correctly are all prerequisites for developing a kayaking finesse. The best boaters are fanatics about their strokes, practicing and fine-tuning them on flat, easy water.

All strokes are based on two important principles. First, your torso, not your arms, is the primary source of power. Second, a secure hold on the paddle shaft is necessary before making any stroke movement.

Think of your torso as the engine, your arms as the transmission, and your paddle blade as the wheels. Too often paddlers use their arms as the engine and don't have a smooth transmission of power. The result is tired arms and ineffective strokes.

TECHNIQUE TIP

Does your boat have a rudder? Practice these strokes with the rudder up, or disengaged, to learn the full impact of boat control.

A secure hold on the paddle shaft includes grasping the shaft fully in the control hand, as if you are picking up a glass of water. Then grasp the shaft with the second hand, with all fingers wrapping around the shaft, knuckles aligned with the control hand. Thumbs grasp the shaft on the side opposite the knuckles.

Finally, are you "wearing" your kayak? Think of seven points of contact when sitting in your boat: two feet, two knees, buttocks, and both hips. Each contact point helps you control your boat and generate optimum performance and control. Boat outfitting using blocks of foam and duct tape can help customize a "loose fit." Make sure you can still wet exit freely after making any outfitting adjustment.

We start with sweep strokes, which turn the boat and help you control your direction. Then we study the forward stroke and some tricks for keeping the boat going straight. Draw strokes to move sideways and reverse paddling round out our strokes lesson.

Forward Sweep

A well-developed forward sweep stroke enables you to reach your paddling potential. Used to turn the boat, forward sweep strokes incorporate three principles: (1) They are powered by large muscle groups of the torso, (2) they follow a full 180-degree arc, and (3) they require a solid plant of the blade into the water.

The powerful muscles that connect your torso to the lower body power this stroke, while arm muscles are reserved for small, subtle adjustments. Torso rotation enables you to harness this large muscle group. Do this by turning your torso and extending the blade forward. Straighten the arm near the water, and pull your other hand back and below your shoulder. Plant the blade completely in the water, then unwind your torso. As you reach the end of comfortable twisting, lift the edge of the boat on the side of your stroke by lifting your knee as you drive your forward hand across the deck of the boat (figure 6.8).

Figure 6.8 Forward sweep stroke.

TECHNIQUE TIP

Many sea kayaks have rudders that can be steered using foot controls. To use the rudder to assist with a gradual turn, push on the left pedal to turn left. For a tight turn you will not use the rudder. Instead, you tilt the boat way up on edge, away from the direction of the turn, while using sweep strokes.

During the sweep, the blade should travel in an arc extending about 3 feet (.9 meter) from the boat (figure 6.9). To do this, both hands should start below shoulder level. Make sure the top of the blade remains submerged throughout the stroke. To maintain your torso rotation, watch your blade sweep all the way to the back. Pay close attention to ensure the blade angle stays straight up in the water. Without your adjustment by cocking your wrist, the blade has a tendency to twist at the end of the stroke, reducing its bite on the water.

How you apply power is important as well. Yanking the paddle simply pulls it through the

Figure 6.9   Forward sweep stroke.

water. A solid hold on the paddle allows it to move effectively. Bubbles or splashes behind the blade are an indication that you are pulling too fast. Keep the blade perpendicular in the water. A common mistake is to hold the paddle at an angle where the blade is like a scoop, lifting the water. This angle simply lifts water and doesn't move the stern around. To correct this, punch across your body with your top hand, twist your torso with the stroke, and watch the blade as you pull all the way into the boat at the stern. Notice how well your boat turns when the blade grabs the water securely.

A good fit in your boat ensures that the power from the stroke is transferred into your boat with your legs, by pushing on the sweeping side's foot peg and pulling your hip toward the blade. Practice forward sweep strokes both while the boat is flat and while it's on edge.

The last part of the sweep stroke is so important and so frequently botched that instructors often isolate it by calling it a stern draw. For the purposes of practice, it's important to move your sweep stroke in a full 180-degree arc from bow to stern. But often you will vary the length of the sweep to provide the turn needed. For instance, the back portion of the sweep is used to pull the stern around without moving the boat forward. This is the stern draw.

Reverse Sweep

Occasionally, for a quick turn, you will use a reverse sweep (figure 6.10). This is simply the opposite of the forward version (figure 6.11). Use the back of the blade, and provide most of the power while your torso unwinds. Linking the two strokes, one on each side, can provide a crisp turn. Practice this turn, and critique how smoothly you are doing the motion. This stroke combination is great for turning around.

In a short whitewater boat, you will be able to spin easily and fast enough to get dizzy. In a sea kayak the turn will be slow, like jockeying your car around in a narrow driveway.

Draw Stroke

Occasionally, you'll want to move sideways. A basic stroke for this is the draw stroke (figure 6.12). Turn your torso to place the working blade straight out from your hip. With both hands over the water, hold the top hand in place as you pull in the blade. Tilt your boat away slightly. At the end of the stroke, turn the working blade 90 degrees for an underwater recovery back to the start position for the next draw stroke (figure 6.13).

A sculling draw is a variation of the draw stroke (figure 6.14). It accomplishes the same movement, and it is a good exercise to help you feel the effects of subtle changes in blade angle. Feather the blade along a 2-foot (.6 meter) line 6 inches (15 centimeters) away from your boat, making sure to keep the shaft straight up and down. Gradually

Figure 6.10 Reverse sweep.

Figure 6.11 Reverse sweep.

Figure 6.12 Draw stroke: *(a-c)* front view and *(d-f)* side view.

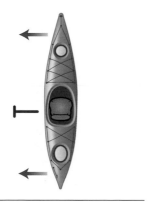

Figure 6.13 Draw stroke.

Figure 6.14 Sculling draw.

open the blade angle on the forward portion of the stroke, then switch it so the leading edge is open as you bring the blade back. Don't pull in on the blade or apply too much force; instead, think of it more like making a figure 8 in the water using both edges of the working blade. Your goal is a maximum sideways pull on the boat, with a minimum resistance to moving the blade. Done correctly, the sculling draw moves the boat sideways with great control and finesse.

Going Forward

When you first tried paddling forward, you probably used your small, nimble arm muscles to provide all your power. A better strategy is to incorporate larger muscles for a more powerful, efficient stroke.

Sound familiar? As in sweep strokes, forward strokes depend on power that originates from torso rotation. The challenge is keeping the blade vertical to the side of the boat, which results in an efficient pull forward. The blade in a forward stroke should be very close (2 to 3 inches) to the boat, with your top hand remaining at eye level. This blade position minimizes the turning effect resulting from a wide blade arc. Remember, the farther away the blade is positioned, like a sweep stroke, the more the boat will turn.

Torso rotation is easily learned while on land, in front of a mirror. Using a pole approximately 3 feet (.6 meters) long, sit on the floor facing a mirror, gripping the pole like a paddle held shoulder height in front of you. Practice the forward stroke technique as described. This drill allows you to monitor how much you are rotating and to feel the rhythm of movement without having to deal with keeping your boat stable or straight.

Let's look a little more closely at the hand positions for a forward stroke. Equally skilled paddlers enjoy endless debates on the merits of a power stroke with a high top hand and a touring stroke with both hands kept low.

For short boats, short distances, and high speeds, people tend to paddle with a shorter paddle, allowing a higher shaft angle. The top hand remains high between shoulder and eye level. For shorter sprints, such as dealing with surf, you need this power forward stroke.

For extended paddling, the forward stroke is a little more cyclical; the top hand drops, elbows drop, and the stroke comes back a little farther in lieu of getting extended toward the front. In the touring forward stroke, the biomechanics of propelling the boat become secondary to reducing the effort you need to expend. To paddle long distances, you will find lots of stroke variations and explore different ways to keep the boat moving.

To begin the stroke, lead with your chest—the bigger the twist the better (figure 6.15). Get extra blade extension by bending your top arm. Concentrate on getting the blade crisply and fully submerged in the water before pulling yourself forward. Use the power of your leg and torso muscles before allowing your bottom arm to bend. Push on the foot brace for extra power. Strive to find a smooth, gliding sensation, without any front-to-back bobbing. Pull the blade out as it reaches your hip, and wind up for the stroke on the other side (figure 6.16).

Figure 6.15 Forward stroke.

Going Straight

Paddling in a straight line may be your first frustration in kayaking. The boat may seem to have a mind of its own, twisting into tighter and tighter turns with each stroke. Although a sea kayak's rudder helps the paddler follow a straight path, certain strokes are useful to maintain the line.

When the boat starts to turn, it can be corrected with a solid sweep or stern draw. Be sure to line up on a distant landmark so you realize earlier that the boat is turning. With experience, you will anticipate a turn and correct it before the boat starts to spin. Don't waste energy trying to correct it by making stronger forward strokes.

Figure 6.16 Forward stroke.

PADDLING IN MOLASSES

Speed from a standstill is the key to kayaking all waters. Think of your boat as gliding in a giant vat of molasses. Each stroke will stick securely in the water to carry the force it needs to move you quickly and efficiently. By imagining the blade pulling against molasses, you will use the force needed to effectively pull the boat forward.

The blade in molasses analogy can provide the answers to commonly asked questions about the length and speed of forward strokes. The blade should be planted as far forward as your torso twist allows, in order to pull yourself forward the greatest distance. Don't pull until the blade is fully immersed. When the blade reaches your hip, the power phase of the stroke is completed and the recovery begins. Simply increasing your stroke rate won't necessarily make your boat go faster. To go faster, concentrate on pulling harder while keeping the blade in the water, then recover quickly to the next blade plant.

Reverse Paddling

Important for stopping, moving backward, and other maneuvers, reverse paddling complements your other strokes. Without changing your grip, use the back face of the blade and the same techniques for forward paddling except in reverse (figures 6.17 and 6.18).

Figure 6.17   Reverse stroke.

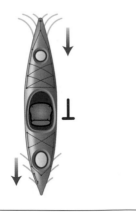

Figure 6.18   Reverse stroke.

Bracing

The brace is a defensive maneuver that can keep you right side up. The blade rests (or slaps) on the water to allow a hip snap to right the boat. A brace requires a fair amount of paddle dexterity and timing, so don't be surprised if you learn to roll first.

A common misconception is that leverage, getting your head up, and pressure on the blade are the keys to a good brace. This is all wrong! Easy braces require that you keep the shaft horizontal and slide the blade in close to the boat to make it easy to slide your weight over the boat. Move the blade inboard, closer to the boat, to help center your weight over the boat.

Low Brace

When you watch someone making a successful low brace, it may appear that the paddle brings the boat right side up. This isn't quite right. The paddle offers only momentary support while your torso and knee motion rights the boat. For a low brace you use the back, or nonpower, face of the blade. Your elbows are directly above your hands.

High Brace

A good high brace commits your body to the water, with your elbows low and a minimum of force on your shoulders and blade. Your hands are directly above your elbows. Throw your head to the water to exaggerate the hip snap motion, and curve toward that side. Then, to recover, you can slink your body and head up over the upright boat.

For safe and effective braces, your hands shouldn't move more than a couple inches (a few centimeters) from your shoulders. Your elbows should act like shock absorbers, so keep the shaft in front of your shoulders. Use smooth finesse rather than power. Overextension of your arms in an attempt to get more leverage makes rolls and braces harder because it pulls your head and torso off-center. Plus it exposes your arm and shoulder to injury. The safe finishing position for braces and rolls is with your elbows low and in close to your body. Don't worry if you don't save yourself with a brace. Equally important are good self-rescue skills covered in chapter 5.

Customized Strokes

The third level of strokes is customized strokes. To a casual observer, customized strokes may look like basic or compound strokes, but they are different. Two significant variations differentiate customized strokes from basic or compound strokes.

First, the motion of the paddle through the water is something other than those pictured as pure strokes in this chapter. For example, the motion of travel of the pure form of a draw stroke is at a right angle to the center of the kayak. No rule prohibits a paddler from doing a draw stroke at a 45- or 60-degree angle to the boat or from moving the draw toward the bow or stern of the kayak.

The second characteristic of a customized stroke is that the blade often travels through the water at an angle other than a right angle to the motion of travel. This concept is typified by the stationary draw and the stationary push-away. In the stationary draw, the motion of the kayak through the water hits the blade at an angle that has the effect of pulling the kayak toward the blade.

TECHNIQUE TIP

Imagine sitting in your boat and reaching forward to start a lawn mower. This twisting reach is the source of the torso and hip power needed for kayaking. However, using that power is tricky. Too much front-to-back motion bobs the boat and jeopardizes your control and efficiency. Instead, use torso rotation, twisting around your spine to provide the pull of each stroke.

To practice these concepts with your forward stroke, try flatwater paddling alongside a series of fixed points such as dock pilings or buoys. The blade should enter the water cleanly, with minimal splash. Watch the blade, and monitor how much it slips with each stroke. It should hardly move at all, while you move past. You should consistently feel resistance against the blade. Remember the boat in molasses analogy!

The easiest way to develop your customized paddling skills is to use paddling drills that require you to maneuver in reference to fixed objects such as a dock, buoys, or gates. Paddlers learn quickly that to make the kayak go where they want it to go in relation to the fixed object, they must adjust and vary their strokes. The use of gates, docks, and other reference points provides immediate feedback.

To practice the strokes described in this chapter and to give paddlers an opportunity to work on linking strokes and creating compound strokes, the following drills and maneuvers can be used in a confined, protected area close to shore. These drills are typical exercises that learners and instructors can use to develop customized strokes and skills. When performing dock drills, be aware of other boaters and people fishing in the area.

Docking Drills

A dock provides a convenient reference point. Approach the dock at a right angle, and then use forward and reverse sweeps to turn so that the kayak is sideways, adjacent to the dock (figure 6.19). Use reverse strokes to stop the forward momentum if needed. Practice approaching the dock from both right and left turns. The approach and stop should be well controlled, with minimal splashing. Do not ram the dock!

Try a **circle drill** where you paddle clockwise and then counterclockwise around a float. Start with a wide circle and then narrow its diameter. This drill is useful in developing the forward-with-correction strokes (figure 6.20).

The **sideways dock drill** is another drill to try. With the kayak parallel to the dock, move the kayak away from the dock using a series of draws or sculling draw strokes (figure 6.21a). The objective is to keep the kayak parallel with the dock. Then move the kayak back toward the dock. Keep the strokes smooth and graceful.

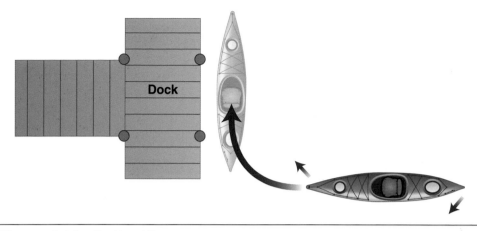

Figure 6.19 Docking drill.

Unlike the sideways dock drill, in the **right-angle dock drill** you orient your kayak perpendicular to the dock, and move the kayak alongside next to the dock. The objective is to keep the kayak perpendicular to and the same distance from the dock as it moves (figure 6.21*b*).

The **sideslip drill** with the dock is an excellent drill for learning the stationary draw. A paddler learns the effect of changing the blade angle of the stationary strokes and the importance of where the stroke is placed in terms of the kayak and the paddler.

Using the dock as a reference point, paddle parallel to the dock and then sideslip the kayak toward the dock, keeping the kayak parallel to the dock as the kayak sideslips (figure 6.22). To sideslip, use a stationary draw. Flip the drill around and approach from the other direction, using a stationary draw on the other side.

Wiggle Course

A wiggle course uses single buoys to create a series of maneuvers for the learner. For example, two buoys can be placed the length of the kayak plus 2 to 3 feet apart. Paddle the kayak sideways through the buoys without touching them (figure 6.23). Using the same setup, you could paddle a figure 8 through the buoys. You can also perform a series of turns, sideslips, and other maneuvers through a series of several buoys (figure 6.24).

SAFETY TIP

If you have shoulder problems, seek experienced instruction to help you learn the brace and roll. If you don't have shoulder problems, seek experienced instruction to help you avoid shoulder problems!

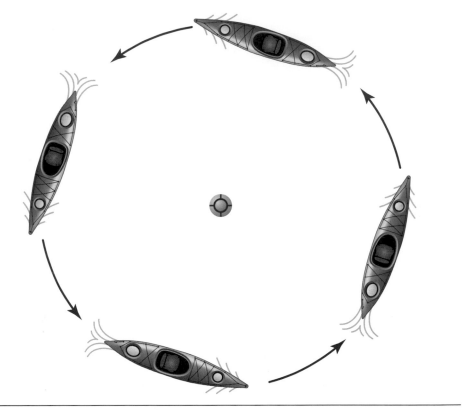

Figure 6.20 Circle drill.

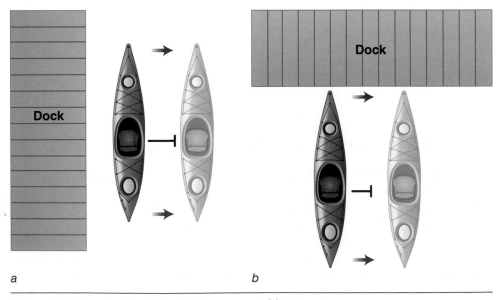

a

b

Figure 6.21 Docking drills: *(a)* sideways and *(b)* right angle.

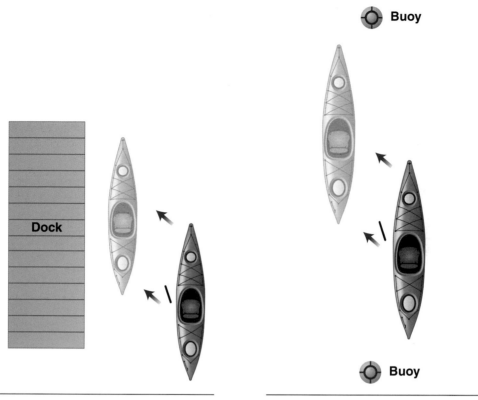

Figure 6.22 Sideslip drill.

Figure 6.23 Two buoy wiggle course.

Gates

Derived from racing, gates provide the kayaker the challenge of maneuvering both the bow and stern through the gate without touching it. Useful primarily for river and whitewater boats, a simple four-gate course can provide almost an infinite variety of skill drills (figure 6.25). The use of gates requires great precision on the part of the paddler as they also require specific paddle placement to avoid hitting the gates with the paddle. Gates can be hung under a bridge or from a wire stretched across a body of water.

Rescue and Emergency Protocols

Kayaking is a "get wet" sport. View rescues as part of the activity, and have fun learning how to do them in pools or warm-water situations. You should know and practice a full repertoire of rescues. Practice on warm water and calm conditions, so you'll gain confidence in your rescue ability, but be prepared for the initial shock of hitting the cold water during an outing. Take a class to learn some of the finer points of rescues and to get valuable feedback on your form. Most rescue techniques are easiest when done correctly, and an instructor can point out the nuances of good technique. Don't even think that you know it from simply reading and looking at the pictures!

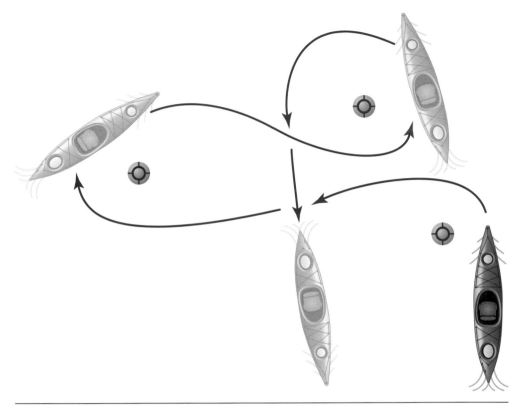

Figure 6.24 Sample wiggle course with more than two buoys.

Self-Rescue

If you capsize close to shore in calm water, first signal others to let them know you are OK. Hang on to your gear, especially your paddle and boat. If possible, roll your boat upright to make it easier to tow. Place any stray gear inside. If you are close to shore, you may choose to tow your boat. Tow your kayak with your end lines, and swim using a strong scissors kick (figure 6.26).

If you capsize in moving water in a river, assume a defensive position by lying on your back with your legs pointing downstream. Arch your back to stay as close to the surface as possible, and avoid bumping the bottom. Keep your feet on the surface to help avoid one of the most common river hazards, foot entrapment (see page 98 and 188).

Angle your head toward the closest safe shore, and backstroke to safety. If you are being swept rapidly toward a hazard, you may need to roll to your side into an aggressive swimming position to reach safety more quickly, but stay flat along the surface until you reach shallow, slow water.

Hold your boat and paddle with one hand and swim with the other if it is safe to do so. Otherwise let go of your gear and take care of yourself first.

If swimming in surf, push your boat in front of you toward shore so the boat is carried ashore first.

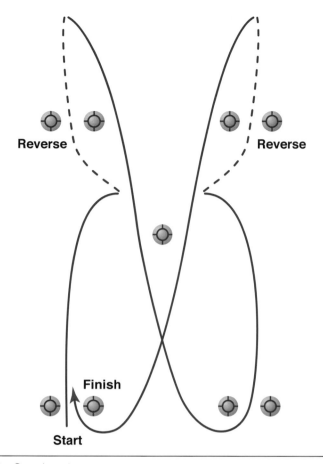

Figure 6.25 Sample gate sequence.

Figure 6.26 Self-rescue.

Paddle Float

One of the most important rescue systems works reliably in calm water and without outside assistance. However, you will need a float for the end of your paddle. This method is easiest with deck rigging to hold the paddle float in position as an outrigger (figure 6.27).

After the swim, hang onto your boat with a leg in the cockpit. This frees both hands to attach the paddle float to the blade and inflate. At this point flip the boat upright, and position the paddle into the rigging, perpendicular so it can be an outrigger. Then kick with your legs to plane your body out before lunging your chest onto the stern deck. Slide one leg in then the other before turning toward the paddle float to establish a sitting position. These steps keep your center of gravity low throughout the rescue to avoid flipping. At this point, a bilge pump can empty the water from your boat so you can continue on your way.

If you don't have rigging, position the paddle shaft behind the cockpit rim so your hand can grasp both the paddle shaft and cockpit rim. Once your chest is up over the boat, you reposition the hands to maintain the paddle float support.

A stirrup (sling) to assist your reentry to the boat is an option. A paddle float made of foam is the preference of paddlers in very cold regions, where cold hands and shock make it difficult to inflate a float.

Water-emptying techniques can save pumping time but keep you in the water a little longer. A popular method to empty the water involves positioning yourself at the bow and doing a strong scissors kick to help lift the bow before flipping the boat right side up.

Figure 6.27 Paddle float rescue.

Boat-Assisted Rescue

A self-rescue is often the quickest and safest method for a swimmer to reach safety, but a paddler can assist a swimmer in several ways. The simplest method is to paddle over to the swimmer and instruct him to hold on to either the bow or stern of your boat. Both towing and pushing a swimmer work well, but determining which will work best in a given situation requires practice.

If towing is called for, have the swimmer hold on to the grab loop, end line, or handle at the stern. Instruct the swimmer to kick and swim (to help forward progress) and to stay close to the surface for safety. Paddle to the closest safe shore.

When pushing (bulldozing) a swimmer, have the person hold on to the bow and wrap his or her legs up around the hull. Then paddle to shore. This technique works especially well with panicked or tired swimmers.

Bulldozing an empty boat to shore can work too, although you'll notice the boat will not follow directions well (figure 6.28a). You can also tow a kayak (figure 6.28b). Again, practice is crucial. To rescue a paddle, simply pick it up and place it in your boat, or hold the shaft alongside your paddle shaft and paddle forward (this takes practice). You might also use a sling to tow the paddle, or secure it in your deck rigging on a sea kayak.

Figure 6.28 Boat-assisted rescue: *(a)* bulldozing and *(b)* towing.

Raft-Reenter-Pump

The most common assisted rescue occurs when the rescuing paddler pulls alongside the swamped boat to stabilize it for reentry. To help expedite the rescue process, the rescuer should always assert himself with clear directions for the swimmer.

Kayaks first get positioned side by side so paddlers can hold on to each other's cockpit rims (figure 6.29). Positioning this way, called "rafting up," allows a paddle to span the kayaks, creating greater stability. The rescuer leans over and grabs the cockpit to provide the necessary stability. Use the bow-to-stern stabilizing position. This is the basic rescue position used in many rescues. Note how important it is to keep contact with your paddle and boat. After the swimmer is safely back in his kayak, he can pump the water out.

Figure 6.29 Raft-reenter-pump.

TECHNIQUE TIP
Self-Rescue

Just for grins, try climbing back into your capsized boat in deep water with no assistance. Trying this will quickly make you understand the benefits of some other rescue systems. This practice is especially important because it reminds you of the safety advantages of paddling in a group.

Shore-Based Rescue

Ropes can be a useful tool for helping swimmers reach shore. Throw ropes can be stored in a throw bag designed for quick and easy deployment or coiled securely in an area where the paddlers will not be entangled in the event of a capsize. In either case, the rope itself should float and be brightly colored for easy visibility. Because of their simplicity and speed of operation, throw bags are recommended.

Usually between 50 and 70 feet (15 and 20 meters) long, these devices are such important tools that every paddler should carry one. Regular practice with the throw bag is necessary to develop speed and accuracy.

To use a throw bag, first make sure your footing is secure. Open the bag to allow the rope to run out freely, and then grasp the bag in your throwing hand. Hold the free end in your other hand. Shout out to the swimmer. The accepted call is "Rope!" Then throw the bag either overhand or underhand, whichever works best for you in practice. Aim to cross the swimmer with the rope by throwing the rope bag past the swimmer (figure 6.30). Then steady

Figure 6.30 Shore-based rescue using a throw bag.

yourself for a significant force when the rope becomes taut. Sitting down or having another person help you hold steady is a good idea. Pendulum the swimmer (once the rope is pulled taut, the swimmer will swing to your side of the river) into a safe location, or pull the person closer if you must help her avoid a downstream hazard. Warn the swimmer to stand up only in water that is knee deep or shallower.

All paddlers should be able to swim with a life jacket on and be able to assist a swimmer with either a boat-based rescue or a rope thrown from shore. These skills are essential. Advanced skills, such as wading, either singly or in groups, to rescue entrapped paddlers or pinned boats can be helpful. Being able to set up mechanical systems to rescue people or equipment, swim in difficult conditions, and swim safely over a strainer can be vital for the river paddler. Paddlers on lakes and rivers should learn the necessary rescue and safety skills (and more) in a class setting taught by knowledgeable, experienced, certified instructors. Go to www.americancanoe.org for information about ACA instructor certification.

Other Assisted Rescues

If a swimmer is close, offer a paddle to pull the person to safety. If you are on shore, you can extend branches or boats into the water to offer assistance.

Deep-Water Assists: Kayak-Over-Kayak Rescue

If one boat capsizes in deep water, a second boat can provide rescue assistance without the need to move to shore. The following are general steps for this quick and effective boat-assisted rescue:

1. The capsized paddler positions himself at the end of the overturned kayak (see figure 6.31).

2. The rescue boat takes a position at the end of the swamped boat, forming a "T."

3. The swimmer at the end of the swamped kayak pushes down on the end. The rescuer lifts the other end out of the water, twisting the kayak slightly to break the suction.

4. The rescuer pulls the boat across her deck, balancing it at the midpoint and allowing it to drain. As the boat is pulled in, the swimmer moves to the end of the rescuer's boat and holds on.

5. The rescuer rolls the boat upright and slides it back into the water, being careful to maintain contact and control. The boat is positioned parallel to the rescue boat, the rescuer holding onto its cockpit to stabilize it.

6. The swimmer moves to the side of his boat and, using a scissors kick and arm strength or with assistance of a rescue sling, reenters the boat. Once the paddler is positioned safely back in his boat with a paddle, the rescue boat can let go.

TANDEM BOAT: ASSISTED AND SELF-RESCUE

Tandem rescues have slight modifications. In using the T-rescue for a tandem boat-assisted rescue, two paddlers can provide the support necessary for lifting the swamped boat and emptying the water. To stabilize the boat, grab the bow cockpit rim. If self-rescuing in a tandem kayak, paddlers first position themselves on opposite sides, and each stabilizes the kayak for the other to reenter. The first paddler in uses the sculling low brace (see chapter 6 for strokes) for stability while the second paddler enters.

Figure 6.31 Kayak-over-kayak rescue.

Rescue Sling

A method that enables a paddler to climb into a boat with little difficulty is the rescue-sling technique. Loop over the side of the kayak a section of line or webbing long enough to hang into the water. Fasten the loop on a paddle that is "locked" under both boats. The paddler then places a foot in the loop, using it like a stirrup. Lifting the hips above the top of the deck, the paddler climbs onto the back deck, lying on her abdomen. Placing both feet and legs into the boat under the front deck, the paddler rolls over and into the seat. The boat continues to be stabilized by the rescue boat sitting parallel.

Rolling

The Inuit developed the roll as a lifesaving move in freezing waters, hence the term *Eskimo roll*. Modern-day recreational paddlers use the same move as a convenient self-rescue on friendlier waters. During remote touring trips or on difficult water, the roll can still be a lifesaver. Knowing how to roll will help you avoid inconvenient and unnecessary wet exits. Whether you are a long way from shore or are being swept downstream on a river, the presence of mind required for a roll is worth it. You don't stay immersed as long, so you stay warmer and can quickly continue on your way.

No maneuver in kayaking intrigues beginning paddlers as much as the roll. For most, the challenge of learning the move intensifies its mystique. Some paddlers learn to roll in one lesson. Others take weeks.

The instructions for this roll are broken into several parts. In the first part, you'll learn how to do the hip snap without the paddle while your body remains out of the water. Then we'll work on the roll while you're underwater holding a paddle.

SAFETY TIP

The importance of paddling in a group can't be overemphasized. A group of paddlers well practiced in rescue skills can deal successfully with many threatening conditions. First, know that starting the trip with a group isn't enough to keep you safe. Paddlers travel at different speeds, the natural outcome of their varying skills and interests. However, before the trip, every member should commit to reuniting with the group at specified stops along the way. Buddy systems are especially helpful when a novice paddler is paired with a veteran of the sport. Some groups work well with a trip leader experienced with the area, along with a sweep boat to follow at the end. Stay within communication distance of your companions.

TECHNIQUE TIP

Concentrate on minimizing the force on the blade. Somehow this is a hard concept for us to remember underwater. Instead of pulling the paddle down, think of following the blade with your upper body.

Hip Snap

The objective of every good roll is to move the boat right side up first, so your body can follow. The key is doing this with little support from the paddle. Minimizing paddle involvement in the roll depends on a solid hip snap in which the torso and knee motion rights the boat.

The best way to practice the hip snap is in the boat along the side of a pool or low deck. Have a partner help you with this exercise. A qualified instructor is the best assistant.

To wind up for a hip snap, relax your torso so the boat flops over on you, almost upside down. Then follow through by gently pressing your right ear toward your shoulder and tugging up on your right knee. Your left knee relaxes, barely even touching the deck. You should have almost no pressure on the left foot pedal. If you are hanging on the boat with both knees, you defeat the hip action, and the entire motion will feel strained. Think of the pressure changing from one side of your bottom to the other. Practice rotating the boat through a full 180-degree range of motion, from upside down to right side up.

This motion should feel very natural before you try rolling with a paddle. Note how little effort it takes to right the boat when you keep your weight floating near the surface and rotate the boat up with your hips, knees, and torso. Think light. Be sure not to push your body up with your arms or lift your head.

To become better acquainted with the body's position in a roll, turn your boat over while your partner stands behind your cockpit holding your torso out to the right while your head remains just above the water's surface. Practice your hip snap from this position.

Rolling Variations

There are actually a number of variations of rolling. We will look at two, the C-to-C roll and the sweep roll.

C-to-C Roll

The essence of the C-to-C roll is the same as the hip snap. The curvature of the torso from one side of the kayak to the other rights an upside-down kayak (figure 6.32).

Figure 6.32 The C-to-C roll.

To start a roll, first capsize the boat and get in the protected forward tucked position, called the setup. Tuck tight. Place your paddle with the power face of the blade up and the shaft parallel to the left seam line. Your wrists will be on the left side of the boat.

Your torso has to lead the arm motion. Any roll you do will rely on positioning the paddle with your torso more than your arms. Open up your body, and arch your back to roll your torso out to your left side. This gets you really wound up into position for a hip snap. Then relax the knee that pulled you into the windup, and rotate the boat up with your hip snap.

Sweep Roll

In the the sweep roll, the righting action occurs while the paddle sweeps to perpendicular. To initiate the sweep roll, the tucked setup position is necessary with the paddle oriented with the powerface "up" and in a slightly climbing position (the edge of the blade away from the kayak must be higher than the closer edge). As the paddler sweeps the paddle to a perpendicular position to the kayak, a simultaneous hip snap brings the kayak upright and under the paddler.

Once you have learned the roll, practice it hundreds of times on flatwater. Decide deliberately to stay in your boat unless you know of a specific hazard. Don't rush. Wait until you can feel the cold air on your hands in the setup position. Go methodically through the rolling motion. On flatwater you can practice reacting to the rushed sensation of an accidental flip by purposely flipping at high speed or with only one hand on the shaft. Don't use your roll to get in over your head, though, in terms of your overall paddling skill. Being in control is much more fun! Whitewater paddlers and paddlers in the surf, remember to wear your helmet!

Bow Rescues

The hip snap motion is also the foundation for bow rescues, where the rescue boat quickly maneuvers to a position perpendicular to the flipped boat. The upside-down paddler scans for the bow of the rescuing boat and reaches up on both sides to grasp it. Once both hands have a firm grasp of the bow, the position is similar to the hip snap practiced by the side of the pool. Right the boat with a strong hip snap without lifting your head or pushing up with your arms.

This is a fairly common rescue method used in hazard-free water, where an attentive friend or instructor can help you stay in your boat. In sea kayaking, bow rescues are used only as practice, since a sea kayak's limited maneuverability prevents impromptu moving into position.

SAFETY TIP

Lifting your head to breathe is a common mistake in bow rescues, braces, and rolls. If the head comes up, the boat stays down. Don't rush to get air. It won't help. Instead, use your head to make effective moves; let it be the last thing to clear the water. This counterintuitive motion involves flexibility and rarely used muscles. Allow plenty of time to practice it!

Summary

It is important to use a good learning progression, first trying easy skills and then moving on to more-difficult ones as you progress. This checklist will help ensure that you learn the sport at a good pace. If you're not accustomed to learning new sports, plan your first kayak experience to be an easy day of just an hour or two. On the other hand, if you are an athletic person, quick to learn different sports, you can have a good full day of it on your first day out.

Checklist for Beginning Paddlers

☐ Take a lesson. Even a two-day lesson can give you a solid understanding of safety and save you from some unpleasant experiences.

☐ Be thirsty for information. Ask lots of questions, read books, watch training DVDs.

☐ Try before you buy! Trying equipment and talking to others in your area will help you focus your paddling interests.

☐ Pick your paddling partners carefully. Experts aren't always the best teachers, and rarely is a spouse, boyfriend, or girlfriend the best choice.

☐ Be realistic in appraising your skill and experience level.

Self-Tow Rescue

☐ If you are close to shore, swimming and towing the boat is the easiest way to rescue yourself.

☐ If a line is attached to the boat, grasp it in one hand. If a line is not attached, try to retrieve one from the boat and attach it.

☐ Hold the line with one hand and swim with the other to shore. If no line is available, try pushing the boat and swimming.

☐ Slide the boat up on shore and empty it.

Emptying the Boat on Shore

☐ Boats full of water are incredibly heavy. If possible, get assistance in emptying it.

☐ Stand near the middle of the kayak, grasp the gunwales, and lift up, tilting the kayak away from you. Lift until the kayak can be turned over and completely emptied.

☐ Lift one end to spill out water, then lift the other end. Seesaw the kayak back and forth to complete the task.

Reentry in Water

If the boat is floating sufficiently high, reentry in the water is possible.

Unassisted by a Second Boat

- ☐ If the kayak is upside down, lift the cockpit to right it.
- ☐ Laying flat in the water simultaneously pull up, reach across to the far side of the kayak, and twist your body, flopping into the kayak on your buttocks.
- ☐ Bail/pump out as much water as possible.
- ☐ If your paddle is not available, use your hands to paddle to retrieve equipment or to go directly to shore.

Assisted Reentry

- ☐ The assisting boat pulls up parallel to the capsized boat.
- ☐ If the boat is upside down, the rescuers help the paddler in the water right the boat by pulling on the cockpit as they turn it over.
- ☐ The rescuers help the paddler hold the boat near the cockpit to counterbalance the weight of the paddlers in the water as they pull themselves up from the far side into the boat.

Assisted Towing Rescue

- ☐ The assisting paddler secures a line to the capsized boat or grabs an existing line on the craft. The line may be attached to the towing boat or the waist of the towing paddler (as long as there can be a quick release from the towing paddler's waist or kayak in the event of another emergency or safety situation).
- ☐ The paddler from the capsized craft swims to the far end of the boat and holds on.
- ☐ The paddlers in the rescue boat paddle to shore, towing the capsized boat and paddlers.

Boat-Over-Boat Rescue

☐ Paddler(s) in water and paddler(s) on rescue boat maneuver capsized boat perpendicular to rescue boat.

☐ At least one paddler in the water swims to outermost end of capsized boat to push down and help break suction while paddler(s) in rescue boat lift end over their boat.

☐ All help push capsized boat so both ends are out of water and boat is empty of water.

☐ Rescue paddler(s) turn boat right side up and return it to water parallel with their boat.

☐ Paddler(s) in water reenter boat (see section on assisted reentry).

CHAPTER 7

Sea Kayaking

We are tied to the ocean.
And when we go back to the
sea—whether it is to sail or to
watch it—we are going back
from whence we came.

John F. Kennedy

Sea kayaks can take you to your dreams . . . a secluded unexplored island, access to a view of an eagle's nest, a magical paddle with the dolphins. Whatever your destination, particularly in large lakes and the ocean, you'll need a set of techniques to keep you safe and to keep the trip pleasurable.

Marine Environment

Think about launching a boat off the coast on a beautiful morning, only to find yourself an hour offshore caught in a steady wind blowing you out to sea. As hard as you paddle, you can't seem to make it back. Although this may seem a bit absurd, it has happened numerous times to unprepared paddlers. Pay attention to the marine environment and to prevailing and forecasted conditions.

Wind

Particularly in touring and sea kayaking, where the paddler is exposed to expanses of open water (fetch), wind is usually the biggest factor to be concerned with. Wind causes two problems for the kayaker. First, a wind coming from any direction, except head-on, tends to weathervane the boat, sweeping it sideways toward the destination. This not only throws the boater off course but also makes the kayak feel less stable since the boat is being pushed sideways across the water. Headwinds make paddling and judging the time required to make a certain distance very difficult. Tailwinds, however, can be a paddler's friend, as long as the winds continue directly along your route.

Winds over 10 knots (11.5 miles per hour; 18.5 kilometers per hour) make paddling too difficult for the beginner, even with an easy-to-access landing beach (figure 7.1). Directional control is lost, and the waves generated by

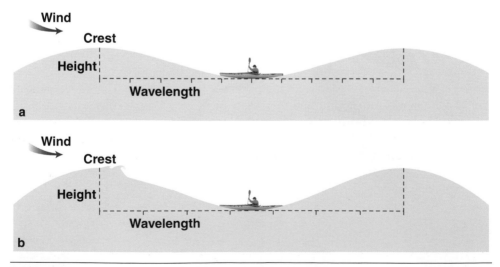

Figure 7.1 Anatomy of a wave. (a) The length of this wave is greater than 6 times its height (10 times). Normally, it will not break and form whitecaps. (b) The length of this wave is 6 times its height. With a wind, it will normally break and form whitecaps.

wind create another hazard. Winds of 10 to 15 knots (11.5 to 17 miles per hour; 18.5 to 27 kilometers per hour) can be identified by the size of waves they make, 1 to 1.5 feet (.3 to .5 meter) tall.

Winds of even 5 miles per hour (8 kilometers per hour) affect beginner kayakers without training, and wind over 10 miles per hour (16 kilometers per hour) can change paddling conditions dramatically. Wind is what makes waves; the strength of the wind and the time it blows over the expanse of open water (fetch) determine the wave height, and a steady wind even makes its own current. The longer the fetch or distance the waves have been building, the more severe the waves will be (figure 7.2).

High winds are to be avoided unless the paddlers are skilled, experienced, and prepared for them. A 25-knot (29 mile per hour; 47 kilometer per hour) wind blowing across a wide ocean

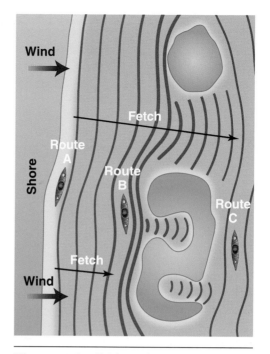

Figure 7.2 Fetch, or the unobstructed distance over which wind travels, influences your route while sea kayaking. A. Most conservative route with smallest waves. B. The largest and most powerful waves with the full effect of fetch. C. Good route until you are traveling between the islands.

expanse for two days will generate waves of 18 feet (5.5 meters). Even relatively low winds will generate potentially hazardous waves when blowing in the opposite direction to current flow. An example of this is wind blowing into a river mouth during an outgoing tide, which will steepen the waves dramatically.

The pressure wind exerts grows geometrically so that a 20-mile-per-hour (32 kilometer per hour) wind exerts four times more push than a wind of 10 miles per hour (16 kilometers per hour). Paddling into a 15-knot (17 mile per hour; 27 kilometer per hour) wind requires twice the effort to maintain speed as paddling in calm; said another way, speed would be cut in half.

Unanticipated wind can wreak havoc on planned trip times, so determining what to expect from the National Oceanic and Atmospheric Administration (NOAA) and other weather predictions, local knowledge, and personal observation is key. If you start to see whitecaps, wind speed is approximately 10 knots (11.5 miles per hour; 18.5 kilometers per hour). The scale most sea kayakers use to relate and estimate wind speed is the Beaufort Wind Scale (table 7.1), which relates sea state to wind speed. You can find wind speed by checking the weather forecast and by carrying and using a handheld wind speed indicator.

Table 7.1 Beaufort Wind Scale

Beaufort number (force)	Speed (mph)	Km/h	Wind description – state of sea – effects on land
0	<1		Calm – mirrorlike – smoke rises vertically
1	1-3	2-6	Light – air ripples look like scales; no crests of foam – smoke drift shows direction of wind, but wind vanes do not
2	4-7	7-11	Light breeze – small but pronounced wavelets; crests do not break – wind vanes move; leaves rustle; can feel wind on the face
3	8-12	12-19	Gentle breeze – large wavelets; crests break; glassy foam; a few whitecaps – leaves and small twigs move constantly; small, light flags are extended
4	13-18	20-29	Moderate breeze – longer waves; whitecaps – wind lifts dust and loose paper; small branches move
5	19-24	30-39	Fresh breeze – moderately long waves; many whitecaps; some spray – small trees with leaves begin to move
6	25-31	40-50	Strong breeze – some large waves; crests of white foam; spray – large branches move; telegraph wires whistle; hard to hold umbrellas
7	32-38	51-61	Near gale – white foam from breaking waves blows in streaks with the wind – whole trees move; resistance felt walking into wind
8	39-46	62-74	Gale – waves high and moderately long; crests break into spindrift, blowing foam in well-marked streaks – twigs and small branches break off trees; difficult to walk
9	47-54	75-87	Strong gale – high waves with wave crests that tumble; dense streaks of foam in wind; poor visibility from spray – slight structural damage

Beaufort number (force)	Speed (mph)	Km/h	Wind description – state of sea – effects on land
10	55-63	88-101	Storm – very high waves with long, curling crests; sea surface appears white from blowing foam; heavy tumbling of sea; poor visibility – trees broken or uprooted; considerable structural damage
11	64-74	102-119	Violent storm – waves high enough to hide small- and medium-sized ships; sea covered with patches of white foam; edges of wave crests blown into froth; poor visibility – seldom experienced inland; considerable structural damage
12	>74	>120	Hurricane – sea white with spray; foam and spray render visibility almost nonexistent – widespread damage; very rarely experienced on land

Tides

Tides offer the kayaker a different type of dynamic paddling environment. Understand tidal waters before venturing onto them. Many of our rivers, all estuaries, and of course the ocean are subject to the rise and fall of tides. The term *tides* refers to the up and down (vertical) movement of water, which is predictably caused by the gravitational pull of the moon and to a lesser extent the sun. Nautical charts reflect the average low tides where they show water depth. These are averages; there are lower low tides and higher high tides, particularly during the full and new phases of the moon.

TECHNIQUE TIP

Tidal height can be predicted by the rule of twelfths, which says that tide height changes 1 twelfth in hour 1, 2 more twelfths in hour 2, 3 more twelfths in hour 3, 3 more in hour 4, and then 2 more in hour 5 to all by hour 6 (1, 2, 3, 3, 2, 1).

The tides in most parts of the eastern United States and most common throughout the world are *semidiurnal*, which means two high and two low tides each day, separated by about 6 hours and 15 minutes. If high tide is at 6:00 a.m., then low tide is at approximately noon.

Along the northern shore of the Gulf of Mexico tides are *diurnal*, or just one high and one low per day. On the Pacific coast, tides are *mixed* because they contain both types, with the typical having a higher high and lower low.

Tidal range is the difference between high (flood) tide and low (ebb) tide. If high tide is 6 feet (1.8 meters) and low tide is zero, the range is 6 feet. These tidal ranges vary from extremes of 50 feet (15.2 meters) to only 2 feet (.6 meter) or less.

For a paddler, this up and down movement means water depth to paddle in. At high tide you may be able to paddle across land that is literally land (too shallow) at low tide. Kayaks don't need much water, but they do need at least 6 inches (15 centimeters), and water below 3 feet (.9 meter) slows speed dramatically, affecting trip-planning time. Some great venues can be visited only at near-high tide.

Tidal Currents

Tidal currents are the in and out (horizontal) movement of the water, affected by the gravitational pull of the moon and sun. Just like the river currents caused by gravity, these currents are like a moving sidewalk going at a barely noticeable speed (drift) or up to as much as 15 miles per hour (24 kilometers per hour) in the most extreme.

The most obvious issue is whether you are paddling with the movement or against it. If you are paddling 3 miles per hour (4.8 kilometers per hour), on a current moving at 2 miles per hour (3.2 kilometers per hour), your total speed

The cure for anything is salt water—sweat, tears, or the sea.

Isak Dinesen

made good is 5 miles per hour (8 kilometers per hour). If you are paddling 3 miles per hour against a current of 2 miles per hour, you would be blazing along at 1 mile per hour (1.6 kilometers per hour). This has quite an impact on trip-planning times. If you are paddling across a current, you will be carried (set) downcurrent unless you take action to counter. *Set* refers to the direction the current is going (e.g., 180 degrees).

For example, if you paddle directly across a 2-mile-per-hour (3.2 kilometer per hour) current at a right angle, at the end of 30 minutes you will be 1 mile (1.6 kilometers) off course. This is countered by either ferrying at an angle to maintain your desired course or paddling upcurrent enough to compensate before crossing (figure 7.3).

In addition to these navigational issues, current can dramatically change the water dynamics. When water is compressed between objects it speeds up, and when it meets resistance it will go around or over what is opposing it. This causes waves, pillows, overfalls, hydraulics, boomers, eddies, and other special features and potential hazards. Such dangers on the water are covered in detail in chapter 8. See the sidebar "ACA Scale of Difficulty for Coastal Waters" for more information.

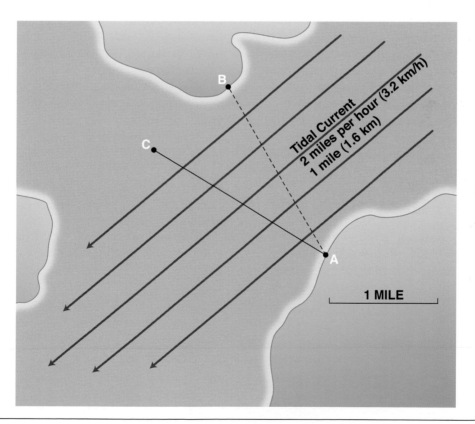

Figure 7.3 Effects of current on travel time. Route A to B is the intended course. With a paddling speed of 4 miles per hour (6.4 kilometers per hour), the total distance traveled is 2 miles (3.2 kilometers) and the time to location is 30 minutes. Route A to C is the uncorrected course after 30 minutes of paddling.

Outgoing tidal current meeting opposing wind is a common occurrence and can steepen waves dramatically. If tidal current passes a point of land or an island, there will be an eddy on the back side, which means opposing streams of water making an eddy line that can capsize unaware or untrained paddlers. As usual, awareness is of primary importance along with the skills to avoid hazards or use features for play.

In addition to tidal currents, special ocean currents such as the Gulf Stream indicate prevailing (or most typical) conditions.

Understanding Tides and Currents

As the tide rises and falls, large volumes of water are redistributed in the sea. The currents that move this water can be very strong and can make returning to shore unexpectedly difficult, often taking you farther than planned. Occasionally, an ebbing tide (as tide goes out) can pose a severe threat because of the speed and power it has to carry you from shore. Tidal current tables, different from simple charts for high and low tides, are available in many coastal areas. Highly detailed tidal current charts are produced for a limited number of regions. Local, experienced paddlers can provide a great source of information on the area's tides.

Tide changes can have a dramatic effect on the difficulty of paddling. Sometimes a low tide leaves a shallow area exposed, making for a much greater distance on the return trip or a nasty slog through mud flats. Tides complicate timing the length of a day trip. Usually, locations where this is true are well known by local paddlers and clearly marked on charts.

More than one camp setup or lunch stop has been unexpectedly swamped by an overlooked tide. This is easy to avoid, though, as coastal communities have readily accessible tide tables that indicate high and low tide as well as the variations to be expected. For instance, in Maine the tidal change can be up to 8 feet (2.4 meters), wreaking havoc on the unprepared.

Kayaking on Coastal Waters

We'll now apply the special concerns of the marine environment along with the safety skills you learned in chapter 5. The American Canoe Association created a scale of difficulty for coastal waters to facilitate safer paddling. This system enables paddlers to assess current conditions and to determine potentially more

TECHNIQUE TIP

Waves coming into shore break or crest where the water depth becomes shallower than the height of the wave. Waves in the ocean overlap each other to amplify and offset each other's size, creating what is known as "wave sets." Timing the waves' arrival at the breaking zone can help determine the easiest times for landing and launching.

difficult conditions when they plan their trip. As with any system, it is a compromise of the factors. There may always be one factor, such as an impassible surf zone, that potentially increases the actual difficulty of the water. The scale helps paddlers compare the difficulty of different coastal waters.

This system of difficulty for coastal waters builds on the Beaufort Wind Scale. In addition to wind speed and wave height, the scale incorporates the additional factors of fetch (distance wind travels unrestricted across the water), the distance from shore, the difficulty of passing through the surf zone, the current, and self-rescue and rescue of others in the group. It assumes that, in general, all of these factors increase in difficulty together. This may not always be the case.

The scale is changeable, and the same stretch of water can easily change its classification within a short period of time. Several of the factors (e.g., wind speed and waves) are variable and will change with weather conditions. Early in the day, a stretch of water may be perfectly placid; later during the same day, the same body of water may have large whitecaps and large waves. However, the potential fetch, the difficulty of passing through the surf zone, and the distance from shore are planning factors that affect the difficulty of coastal waters regardless of wind speed and wave height. In general, areas that have large fetch are prone to large waves because these areas are not sheltered. Hence, they are generally rated a higher class even though the wind may not be a factor at the time the paddler is actually paddling the stretch of water.

ACA SCALE OF DIFFICULTY FOR COASTAL WATERS

- **Class 1: Easy.** The water ranges from mirror like to small wavelets, with no breaking crests. No current is present. It is relatively easy, requiring beginner-level skills. Beaufort Wind Scale is less than force 3, "calm" or "light breeze" ranging from 0 to 6 knots (0 to 7 miles per hour; 0 to 11 kilometers per hour). The coastline, islands, or other features are relatively sheltered, reducing the effects of fetch. The paddler is close to shore, and no significant surf zone is present. Rescues are relatively easy and may include shore-based rescues.

- **Class 2: Challenging.** The water is somewhat challenging but easy enough for paddlers with some experience. Seas are relatively small, ranging from 2 to 4 feet (.6 to 1.2 meters) in height. Whitecaps will be present if wind speed increases to force 4. Beaufort Wind Scale is force 3 to 4 with a "gentle" to "moderate breeze" ranging from 7 to 16 knots (8 to 18.5 miles per hour; 13 to 29.5 kilometers per hour). Current is absent or minor, 2 knots (2.5 miles per hour; 4 kilometers per hour) or less. The coastline, islands, or other features still reduce the effects of fetch. The paddler is still relatively close to shore, and passing through the surf zone (if surf is present) is easy and fairly straightforward. Visual and audible communications are clear, and keeping the group together is fairly easy. Rescues are relatively easy to perform.

(continued)

(continued)

- **Class 3: Difficult.** The wind and seas begin to get pushy, and good boat-handling skills are required. Seas are moderately large and steep. There may be currents present, ranging from 2 to 4 knots (2.5 to 4.5 miles per hour; 4 to 7 kilometers per hour), near or exceeding the speed of the average paddler. Beaufort Wind Scale is force 5 to 6, "fresh" or "strong wind" between 17 and 27 knots (19.5 and 31 miles per hour; 31.5 and 50 kilometers per hour). Problems associated with fetch are becoming more of a concern. The coastline is farther away, islands are separated by open expanses, and there is more open water present. Passing through the surf zone is more difficult and may be impeded by larger waves or an irregular or rocky coastline that requires some skill and experience to negotiate. Self-rescue and rescue of others in the group becomes more difficult.

- **Class 4: Very Difficult.** Very rough seas are present, requiring advanced paddling skills. Seas are large, chaotic, and steep, with spray and foam flying in streaks off the wave crests. Beaufort Wind Scale may reach force 7, or "moderate gale" winds between 28 and 33 knots (32 and 38.0 miles per hour; 51.5 and 61 kilometers per hour). If currents are present, they may reach speeds up to 6 knots (7 miles per hour; 11 kilometers per hour). The large expanse of water often makes it difficult to reach shore quickly, and passing through the surf zone poses sufficient risks to the paddler that staying in the open water is often a better alternative. Communications within the group is difficult. Paddlers must be self-reliant and may end up on their own. Rescues are difficult and could endanger other paddlers in the group.

- **Class 5: Extreme.** Even expert paddlers are challenged by these conditions. Seas are very steep, and wave crests are beginning to tumble. Dense spray reduces visibility. Beaufort Wind Scale is force 8 to 9 "gale" winds between 34 and 47 knots (39 and 54 miles per hour; 63 and 87 kilometers per hour). If present, currents may exceed 5 knots (6 miles per hour; 9.5 kilometers per hour). The large expanse of water makes it difficult to reach shore in a timely fashion, and passing through the surf zone poses sufficient risks to the paddler that staying in the open water is often a better alternative. Passing through the surf zone is more difficult and may be impeded by larger waves or an irregular or rocky coastline that requires advanced skills and experience to negotiate. Communications within the group is difficult at best, and paddlers are essentially on their own. Self-rescue or the rescue of others in the group is possible but very difficult and could endanger other paddlers in the group.

- **Class 6: Life Threatening.** Class 6 conditions are life threatening and present a serious danger for any paddler, no matter how experienced or skilled he may be. Seas are huge and chaotic, with numerous breaking waves. The sea is white with spray and foam. Beaufort Wind Scale is a force 10 or higher, consisting of "whole gale" to "hurricane" winds of more than 48 knots (55 miles per hour; 88.5 kilometers per hour). Returning to shore through the surf zone is often impractical, extremely difficult, and life threatening. Communication is very difficult to impossible. Paddlers are essentially on their own. Self-rescue or the rescue of others in the group is probably impossible. These are conditions for experts only with full knowledge of the risks involved.

Launching

A well-protected launch zone is the best situation for beginners starting an outing. Look for protection in a small bay where the waves don't crash in. Most public launch areas are in protected bays, easily accessible even at low tide. Private land issues and limited public access complicate the start of a trip in many regions.

When waves are present at the only launch site available, launching a sea kayak in swells can be the most challenging portion of a day trip (figure 7.4). Trying to put on the spray skirt and paddle out with some speed before the next wave crashes on shore is not easy for the beginning paddler. The easiest system involves having the experienced paddler(s) help launch most of the group, and then launching themselves at the end.

Regardless of wave conditions, learn to anticipate wave patterns and sets. Watch how frequently the large waves approach, and see if there is a pattern to when the smallest waves come in. Predicting wave size and travel will be useful in landings as well.

Landing

Finishing the trip in surf can pose a real challenge for you and your equipment. As with launchings, a carefully chosen protected area can make the task much easier. Search for shallow beaches or pebble beaches hidden in rocky shores (figure 7.5). When forced into a surf landing, find a small set of waves, and time your final sprint to cover the most distance in between waves. You will use a method of waiting as you allow waves to pass under you before they start to curl, then accelerate between the waves to pass safely through the break zone.

Figure 7.4 Launching a sea kayak.

Plan to alter your paddling speed to land on shore on the back side of a wave. A friend on shore, ready to help stabilize your quick exit, can make the landing a lot easier.

If you haven't used good timing to avoid the waves during a landing, their curling, crashing crests will quickly turn you sideways. Riding the wave in sideways is an option, but it requires an excellent brace and lean into the wave (away from the beach). Surf kayakers thrive on the excitement of this ride, particularly in shorter, highly maneuverable boats. For most sea kayakers, however, it is extra excitement not appreciated.

Navigating

Nautical charts are a must for long day trips and any open water crossings and can be fun to use on short day trips. Your first trips are likely to be in areas with islands and low coastal relief, so unless you know the area very well, maps are a good thing to have and use. For some regions and trips, you will want the additional land relief features provided by a topographical (topo) map.

Figure 7.5 Landing a sea kayak.

Get the most detailed scale available and a chart case to keep the map protected but accessible. Charts have navigational buoys as well as low tide designations so you know which ledges will be apparent. Tidal current charts combined with tide tables offer a lot of information that can add to the day's enjoyment. Add to the adventure of a short trip by using them to check your progress. Study the chart key, and take a class to more fully understand navigational markings and chart markings (figure 7.6).

With a compass and nautical chart, orient your map with magnetic north, and mark on your chart your desired path. Then, by moving the compass to your desired course, calculate what bearing you will need to follow. Calculate how long the trip should take. Be sure to factor in tidal changes, wind, and your average paddling speed.

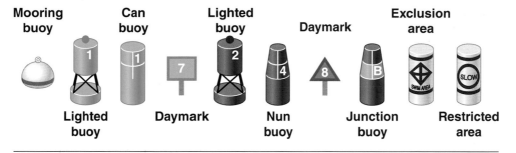

Figure 7.6 Navigational buoys help guide your way.

Strong currents in channel crossings require special strategies to maintain the bearing to your destination. In short crossings, you can think of this as keeping the boat angled slightly into the current to allow a continuous movement forward. This "ferry angle" is borrowed from the old riverboat ferries' means of propulsion across the river. Another option is to depart well upstream of the destination, allowing the current to bring you downstream.

Navigation bearings, landmarks, and triangulation become important skills for all but the easiest of day tours. Some of the best classroom courses on navigation techniques are available from the powerboat safety community. Check out navigation courses offered by the United States Power Squadrons or the Coast Guard Auxiliary.

Every region has its own traits and hazards that only experienced paddlers recognize. Be prepared for them by checking with local shops and outfitters for an appraisal of local conditions. Find out about the kind of currents to expect in channel crossings, the navigation rules with other vessels, the tidal patterns, and updated local weather patterns. Local guidebooks identify hazardous tidal rips as well as notoriously windy and dangerous points.

Share the Waterways

Coastal kayaking often means you will be near other types of traffic, including large boats. Since you are sharing the sea, you need to be aware of navigational rules and proper etiquette.

First you should practice defensive boating. For the kayaker, defensive boating is preventing collisions and mishaps in spite of the actions of others and the conditions around you. Select a route that avoids other boats. Anticipate where larger boats will travel, and avoid those places. Travel outside of the channel or close to shore when the channel extends from bank to bank. Avoid cutting corners that require crossing channels, and when crossing a channel go straight across or at a right angle to the channel. In addition, traveling outside of the main channels and closer to shore is often more scenic.

You also want to see and be seen. Scan the waterway and determine where the other boats are; avoid those places, and keep a safe distance from other boats. Wear bright-colored apparel and life jackets. Use reflective tape and white flare-up lights in reduced visibility. Traveling in groups also increases visibility.

Other Safety Issues

Sea kayaking may seem more benign than whitewater boating, but don't let appearances fool you. Sea kayaking has its own hazards. You learned how to read charts and maps, how to anticipate tides and their resulting effects, and how to anticipate changes in weather. Practicing those skills is the best way to remain safe on the sea. Other safety issues include knowing how to deal with water traffic, being prepared for unexpected weather, being caught by nightfall, and using signaling devices.

Water Traffic

When paddling in areas with other traffic, assume that others can't see you. Also remember that large boats are often less maneuverable. A sea kayak is smaller than most craft, and normal conditions such as glare can hide a boat from easy view. Some paddlers use an orange flag on a tall, flexible pole, the type bicyclists use for visibility. Particularly when crossing shipping and commercial lanes, kayakers should be extra cautious and prompt—minimize the crossing in terms of time and distance. Avoid crossing at tight bends or where there is restricted visibility. The best defense is a carefully planned trip to avoid highly congested areas and times of high traffic.

Weather and Fog

Even with careful planning and attention to weather forecasts, an unexpected storm is likely to catch you sometime in your paddling career. Storms can often move in faster than you can paddle to shore to avoid them. Have alternate plans for landings, and be certain that storms are unlikely before you plan major

SAFETY TIP

Red, right returning. Navigational channels are marked with red (triangular-shaped) and green (square-shaped) markers. When returning to the port or harbor, the red marker is found on the right. These markers mark the main channel used by larger boats. Good etiquette and personal safety suggest that kayakers will normally avoid using this channel.

> The sea, once it casts
> its spell, holds one in its
> net of wonder forever.
>
> *Jacques Yves Cousteau*

crossings. Keeping your group together and knowing rescues can improve your ability to weather the storm. Having a two-way radio or cellular phone can simplify a rescue situation. Learn to recognize the weather changes early, and act accordingly.

Another related hazard is fog. Usually caused by warm air cooling over the water, fog can disorient you, obstruct visual navigation, and prevent larger boats from spotting you. Carry and use a foghorn or whistle in fog situations. Sound the signal to indicate your location every two minutes.

Night Paddling

Although it offers special rewards, night paddling should be avoided until you are equipped with proper lights and navigation skills. Nonetheless, long day trips should include nighttime signaling devices for emergency use. Consult your local outfitter for recommendations for specific styles. Federal and state laws require use of a white light to display in ample time to avoid a collision. Other navigation rules may also apply, such as quickly crossing any shipping or navigation channel to avoid areas where larger boats are restricted in their ability to maneuver.

Signaling Devices

Sea kayakers should always carry signaling devices. They are needed to attract the attention of group members and other craft to avoid a collision and to signal for assistance for a rescue or impending rescue.

Handheld and aerial flares, strobes, and orange smoke canisters are the most common and simplest devices for attracting attention. These pyrotechnic devices must be USCG approved and must not be older than the expiration date stated on the device. Federal and state laws require that a specific number (usually three) be carried for night use. A whistle or foghorn can be used within a group, but only the most robust sound signal can be heard by motorized craft. Waterproof flashlights provide a small margin of safety in the event that your return trip is delayed until after dark. For trips at sea, take backup signaling devices to be safe.

SAFETY TIP
Sea Creatures

The marine environment is full of fascinating and sensitive sea life. Learn about the flora and fauna in the area you are planning to navigate from your local paddling shops and instructors. Take care to protect (and be protected from) the creatures whose home you are visiting.

Summary

Many of the skills discussed in this chapter are kinesthetic skills, or require experience to apply, so simply reading about them is only the first step of your learning process. Kayakers need to have good boat control, good judgment, and well-practiced techniques for dealing with sea conditions. Learning coastal paddling requires a careful learning progression, best established by an experienced instructor in your area. If you try to complete a trip that is too difficult or too long too soon, you really rob yourself of the opportunity to learn and progress safely. Start with short journeys with experienced friends to ensure an enjoyable sea kayaking experience.

CHAPTER 8

River and Whitewater Kayaking

Oh, this ol' river keeps
on rollin', though,
No matter what gets in
the way and which way
the wind does blow,
And as long as it does
I'll just sit here
And watch the river flow.

*Bob Dylan, "Watching the
River Flow"*

At first glance it looks as if the thrill of whitewater is the pure adrenaline of crashing down through waves and big drops. But that is only part of the thrill. Reading the river, figuring out how your boat will react, then picking your route through what may appear to be chaos becomes a rewarding challenge. Identifying basic river features is an important part of whitewater paddling. This knowledge helps keep you safe and allows you to understand the basic whitewater maneuvers. Learning to read a river's features will help you know its friendliness. This skill takes considerable experience, but in most ideal learning situations all that happens from a misread is you flip or simply bang up on a rock. Refer to chapter 5 for descriptions of different river features.

Paddling on moving water requires a different set of skills and builds on skills obtained on flatwater. It is important to understand the force of moving water. A gallon of water weighs about 8 pounds (3.6 kilograms). The faster water flows, the greater the kinetic energy, or force, it creates. Hundreds, even thousands, of pounds or kilograms of force can be created against a boat hull. What fun! Knowing the characteristics of a moving water environment allows you to develop understanding and respect. What may appear as chaos in a flowing rapid is actually very predictable. Part of the fun of river paddling is knowing how to "capture" the river's energy for a fun ride. In this chapter, we apply the skills learned in chapter 6 (strokes) to moving water. We will look at techniques that play on the river features described in chapter 5.

Whitewater Safety

One component of whitewater safety is knowing how to swim in fast water. Practice swimming on your back, with feet up to the surface and pointing downstream. This safe swimming position helps prevent trapping your feet on the bottom of the river. Your kayak training routine should include learning other aggressive swimming techniques and self-rescue skills. Most important is learning to swim aggressively with a sidestroke to the safest eddy or shoreline.

Also important is learning how to accept help from an experienced kayaker. When appropriate, he will offer the end of his boat to help tow you to shore. Listen carefully to his directions, and help by swim-kicking to assist moving toward safety. You should also learn and practice accepting a rope throw for rescue, as paddlers sometimes station ropes at rescue spots in tricky rapids or to retrieve paddlers stranded in the middle.

Successfully running a difficult river is not always a measure of your improvement. Instead, challenge yourself by making hard moves such as ferries and surfing on easy rivers. Racers and all really good boaters develop their skills this way. Knowing your ability and matching it to appropriate rivers is the best way to ensure safe boating. A whitewater river rating system will help you with this.

The whitewater river rating system classifies rivers from Class I to Class VI. Although the system is often discussed, to get an accurate idea of the difficulty of the run you need to get a full description. This includes information about the

The call of the river
is a complexity of
motion and sound
which extracts from
mere mortals the
wildest diversity of
emotional response.
Awe, dread, tranquility,
devotion, ecstasy.

Page Stegner

nature of the rapids. Are they drop pool or continuous? What is the gradient? How many major rapids are there, and are they easily portaged? Is the river generally thought to be safe or dangerous?

This system is not exact; rivers do not easily fit one category, and regional or individual interpretations may cause misunderstandings. Allow an extra margin for safety when the water is cold or if the river is remote.

RIVER DIFFICULTY CLASSIFICATIONS

- **Class I: Easy.** Fast-moving water with riffles and small waves. Few obstructions, all obvious and easily missed with little training. Risk to swimmers is slight; self-rescue is easy.

- **Class II: Novice.** Straightforward rapids with wide, clear channels that are evident without scouting. Occasional maneuvering may be required, but rocks and medium-sized waves are easily missed by trained paddlers. Swimmers are seldom injured, and group assistance, while helpful, is seldom needed.

- **Class III: Intermediate.** Rapids with moderate, irregular waves that may be difficult to avoid and can swamp an open canoe. Complex maneuvers in fast currents and good boat control in tight passages or around ledges are often required. Large waves or strainers may be present but can be easily avoided. Strong eddies and powerful current effects can be found, particularly on large-volume rivers. Scouting is advisable for inexperienced parties. Injuries while swimming are rare; self-rescue is usually easy, but group assistance may be required to avoid long swims.

- **Class IV: Advanced.** Intense, powerful, but predictable rapids requiring precise boat handling in turbulent water. Depending on the character of the river, it may feature large, unavoidable waves and holes or constricted passages demanding fast maneuvers under pressure. A fast, reliable eddy turn may be required to initiate maneuvers, scout rapids, or rest. Rapids may require "must" moves (maneuvers required of the paddler to run the drop without mishap) above dangerous hazards. Scouting may be necessary the first time down. Risk of injury to swimmers is moderate to high, and water conditions may make self-rescue difficult. Group assistance for rescue is often essential but requires practiced skills. A strong Eskimo roll is highly recommended.

- **Class V: Expert.** Extremely long, obstructed, or very violent rapids that expose a paddler to above-average endangerment. Drops may contain large, unavoidable waves and holes or steep, congested chutes with complex, demanding routes. Rapids may continue for long distances between pools, demanding a high level of fitness. What eddies that may exist may be small, turbulent, or difficult to reach. At the high end of the scale, several of these factors may be combined. Scouting is mandatory but often difficult. Swims are dangerous, and rescue is difficult even for experts. A very reliable Eskimo roll, proper equipment, extensive experience, and practiced rescue skills are essential for survival.

- **Class VI: Extreme.** These runs often exemplify the extremes of difficulty, unpredictability, and danger. The consequences of errors are severe, and rescue may be impossible. For teams of experts only, at favorable water levels, after close inspection and taking all precautions. This class does not include drops thought to be unrunnable but may include drops only occasionally run.

Courtesy of American Whitewater www.americanwhitewater.org

River Maneuvers

Paddlers use specific maneuvers on moving water to work with and not battle against the energy of the river current. Because of the amount of force generated against a boat hull by moving water, paddler strength is no match. Techniques such as ferrying, eddy turns, and peelouts allow the kayaker to capture the river's energy to his or her advantage. The added plus is that these maneuvers are great fun! Practice of these techniques will result in a high level of grace and finesse in your paddling.

Ferrying

A ferry is a maneuver that gets you across the river from an eddy on one side to an eddy on the other side. Although this is practical for running a river, the ferry can also move you into fun surf waves.

To ferry, start in the eddy facing upstream. Position yourself nearly parallel to the eddy line. Then establish a slight angle to the oncoming current, and prepare to speed across the eddy line (figure 8.1). This position is often the most important part of the ferry. It requires paddle control and finesse. Backing up then drawing or sculling may be necessary to move into place. With experience, you will learn to jockey into position.

Once you are positioned close to the eddy line, start looking at the current's direction and speed. The current next to the eddy line has usually been deflected by rocks, so it flows in a different direction than the main flow. Establish an upstream angle to move your boat across the current. Generally, this is a 10- to 45-degree angle to the oncoming current. The angle depends on the speed of the water; the faster the current, the more you'll need to point straight upstream at the 10-degree angle. If you are unsure of the angle, a small angle or pointing straight upstream is more conservative. The goal is to keep your bow from getting pushed downstream as you cross into the oncoming current.

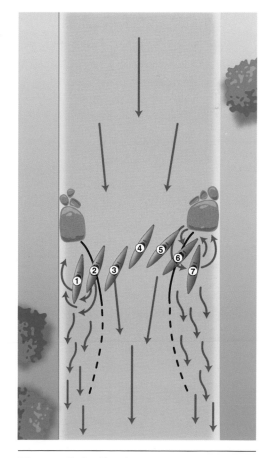

Figure 8.1 Ferrying.

Crossing the eddy line is a crucial point in keeping your ferry angle. The bow is in the current, and the stern is in the eddy, so different forces are acting on your boat. Maintaining good forward speed reduces the time these forces have to alter your course.

Stroke timing and placement are important. The instant your feet reach the oncoming current, you should be poised for a stern-draw correction on the downstream side of your boat, to help prevent your boat from turning downstream. Realize the importance of correcting the angle from the stern when ferrying. The end of the forward sweep, the stern draw, works with the current to turn the boat. The first part of a sweep stroke doesn't correct a ferry angle as well since it pushes the bow against the current.

Another option for correcting the boat angle is a rudder stroke on the upstream side of the kayak. Use good form with the rudder, rotating the blade close to the boat and then pushing away slightly. Set the blade on edge, like a sailboat tiller. This requires rolling your wrists back and a slight counterbalance lean away from the stroke. Don't do an inadvertent braking stroke when you want the easy turn of a rudder. A sloppy, poorly executed rudder stroke slows the boat and makes it tippy.

After you have crossed the eddy line with either a rudder or stern draw, you can open up your angle and paddle directly toward the eddy on the other side of the river. Well-controlled ferries give you the feeling of control on the river.

In a reverse ferry, the boat faces downstream. Reverse ferries are generally used while traveling downstream in midcurrent to view obstacles and determine the best course of travel.

Eddy Turns

Eddy turns are the foundation for controlling the speed of your descent down the river (figure 8.2). In the quiet of the eddy, you can look at the rest of the rapid, rest, and line up for your next move or get out to portage (carry your

PADDLER TIP
Getting Started in the Forward Ferry

Ferrying is a method of crossing current without losing headway downstream. The ferry uses a combination of the water's energy deflected off the side of a properly angled kayak. Proper paddle strokes keep the kayak from moving downstream, while the force of the current provides the "push" to move the boat to the other side of the river.

Start against shore with your boat facing upstream into the current. Angle the upstream end of the boat slightly toward the opposite shore. If the current is slow, angle the boat no more than 45 degrees. If the current is fast, use a smaller angle. Holding the angle, paddle upstream into the current until you reach the other side.

Figure 8.2 Eddy turn.

boat around an obstruction). By paddling into the eddy at the correct angle with a bit of speed, and then tilting the boat up on edge, you'll remain right side up and feel secure.

Boat speed, angle, and lean are key components to entering an eddy. Position the boat so you will cross the eddy line and enter the eddy at a 45-degree angle. The eddy will be a moving target, and it takes practice to get your timing down in order to paddle forward and catch the eddy high to where it is formed at the proper angle.

The proper approach into an eddy gets you there, not a magic set of strokes. This requires setting your approach angle well in advance of the rock and its eddy. Take into account that the current usually bounces off rocks just before the eddy line. This changes the water direction and speed, pushing your bow away from the eddy. By watching the current as it hits the rock and is deflected, the eddy line becomes easier to see (figure 8.3). Study the size and shape of the rock to anticipate the changing current.

Position the boat slightly sideways to the current, keeping the momentum. Sometimes you will need to pause briefly before accelerating into the eddy. Often, it will look as if you are going to hit the rock.

PADDLER TIP

It is important that you paddle forward into the eddy or you will be swept downstream.

Figure 8.3 Approaching an eddy from the paddler's point of view.

Your approach path should land you high in the eddy and deep, away from the eddy line. This will require an aggressive forward speed. If you finish your turn close to the eddy line, or lower in the eddy, where the eddy is less distinctly formed, you'll risk slipping out the bottom. This will make you feel out of control until you spin and find another stopping place.

As you enter the eddy, lean the kayak as you would lean a bicycle through a turn in order to stay balanced. Start leaning into the turn when your feet cross the eddy line. Gradually flatten the boat as you turn upstream. Enter with

PADDLING TIP
Downcurrent J-Lean

When a boat capsizes in moving water, it often happens crossing an eddy line with the boat rolling into the oncoming current. Avoid this by using a J-lean to expose the boat bottom to the oncoming current. The force of water moving faster than a boat can "catch" the hull and roll it out from under an unwary paddler! Anytime a kayak is cutting across current, it is important to keep a slight downcurrent lean on the boat using the J-lean technique—press against your downcurrent buttock while maintaining good upright posture and keeping your nose vertical over your belly button. Proper execution of the J-lean exposes your boat's hull to the oncoming rush of current, allowing water to pass safely under the boat. Lack of a downcurrent J-lean may allow water to "pile" on the upstream side of the hull, resulting in a flip.

enough speed to cross the eddy line, and allow the river current to assist in turning the boat (figure 8.4). If you overpower the eddy speed, you will cut through the eddy and hit the shore or travel out the other side. If you do not have enough speed, you may not make it into the eddy.

Take whatever strokes are necessary to penetrate deep into the eddy. Sometimes a sweep on the downstream side is needed to compensate for the current deflected off the rock. Other times a sweep on the upstream side keeps the boat from turning early. Be sure to allow the bow of the boat to stick into the eddy before initiating a turn.

To summarize the eddy turn:

1. Set your angle of approach.
2. Build (or keep) momentum toward the eddy.
3. Tilt your boat using a J-lean as you cross the eddy line, similar to banking a bicycle through a turn.

Peelouts

A peelout is a way to leave an eddy (figure 8.5). Just like the eddy turn coming in, the technique provides

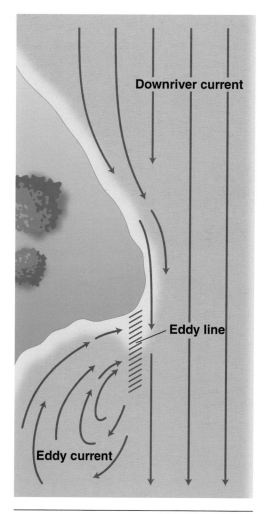

Figure 8.4 The forces of the current help you turn into the eddy.

a safe way to cross the eddy line and use the force and momentum of the river current to carry your boat. Peelouts are sometimes the only safe way to leave an eddy into a powerful jet of water. Boat speed, angle, and lean are key components. You need enough speed to cut across over the eddy line into the oncoming current. Cross the eddy line with an angle between 15 and 45 degrees. The faster the current, the closer you will leave pointing upstream. As the current catches the front half of the boat, the boat will "peel out," turning downstream in the current. Paddle through the turn to make sure the boat is out of the eddy, and continue paddling downstream. A properly executed J-lean keeps the boat upright as it enters the faster current.

Unlike a ferry, which keeps you pointed upstream, peelouts are the moves done to leave an eddy and head downstream. Odds are that your first peelout will be by accident, while trying to cross the eddy in a ferry. Your peelouts from the eddy should be fun and precise. The departure path from the eddy is

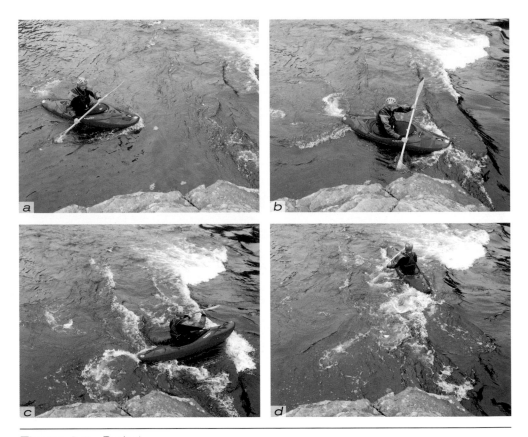

Figure 8.5 Peelout.

almost identical to a ferry but done with just a bit more boat angle relative to the current and eddy line. Use strokes that position the boat and keep it from turning until you've crossed the eddy line.

Peel out of the eddy in the trough of a wave instead of climbing up the back of a wave. If your boat isn't positioned properly for the exit with enough speed, it will be turned rapidly on the eddy line. This is a wobbly place to be.

J-lean downstream while crossing the eddy line. With a J-lean your boat should lean, not you. Lift the upstream knee and ride on one cheek of your bottom. In this position, you will be edging the boat just enough to keep from flipping.

Remember, the faster the current, the greater the J-lean and resulting boat tilt needed to remain balanced. When finishing the turn, gradually shift your weight onto both cheeks to flatten the boat.

Floating Sideways

On occasion, you will position your boat sideways, at an angle to the rapid while running it. This allows you to paddle forward to get to one side of the river and backward to get to the other. Downstream momentum will be lessened as you remain slightly sideways to the current, and the river obstacles won't seem to come at you as quickly. You need to turn straight to avoid the instability of hitting a rock or ledge hole sideways.

Surfing

Forward surfing on a standing wave is really a modification of the forward ferry combined with the force of gravity pulling your boat to the low point of the wave trough. Simply forward ferry into the trough of the wave, then point your boat directly into the current. If the wave is big enough and you have positioned your center of gravity on the upstream side of the wave, you will balance the kayak at a point where gravity will pull you upstream while the current tries to move you downstream. Great fun! Remember to lean downstream if your boat is kicked to one side or the other. Side surfing a big wave is a great way to practice your J-lean.

To surf, look for a wave that starts right next to an eddy. You'll ferry into position so your boat is actually sliding down the wave. The key to getting on a wave is knowing exactly where to aim when leaving the eddy and controlling your boat position in the wave trough.

First, leave the eddy in a ferry. Aim for the depression on the eddy line, in between the peaks of the waves. This is where the trough of the wave meets the eddy.

Position your boat so you are sitting on the wave, with your feet in the trough (figure 8.6). Feel for the sensation of your bow dropping down into the trough. Monitor the distance between the bow and the ramp of oncoming water. Try to skim the bow of your boat along the darker, solid water in the trough of the wave.

When surfing some waves, the water will pour over several inches of your deck; don't let the bow dig in by applying too much power. The bow stays dry while surfing other waves. The instant the bow rises up or slips back, take hard forward strokes to stay on the wave. Keep your boat pointed straight into the oncoming current with stern-draw or light rudder strokes. A well-fitted cockpit will keep water from entering your boat and sloshing around.

PADDLER TIP

"Lean downstream" is the most common advice given to beginner paddlers. Remember, this only applies to maintaining your stability when leaving an eddy. If you leaned all the time, you'd rarely feel balanced! Think of tilting your boat rather than leaning your body.

Enders

Enders are the spectacular air-catching moves of kayaking (figure 8.7). Getting air is as simple as driving your bow upstream into water that is dropping down over steep waves or ledges. This requires very precise surfing skills. Most places for enders have a sweet spot with powerful current to aim the bow. The river power will propel you up into the air. Be ready to roll up!

Loops, Cartwheels, Bow Stalls, and Other Play Boat Moves

Today's play boat designs provide athletic paddlers vessels designed for highly acrobatic moves. These moves grow from mastery of the basic concepts and add yet another degree of drama, fun, and sport to paddling.

Side Surfing

Side surfing is a great way to play on the river and to get an understanding about holes. The goal is to sit sideways in a hydraulic, using the wave shape to hold you in position. You will be free to move if your balance comes from posture and knee lift rather than a heavily weighted paddle, which will make you feel stuck.

Easy side-surfing holes resemble waves with a shallow entry angle on the upstream side. Even a tall wave can offer a gentle ride if its entry is shallow. Initially, avoid such holes as pourovers in which the water moves smoothly

Figure 8.6 Surfing.

back upstream. Where the water falls steeply, a smooth ride is unlikely. In addition, a steep entry angle requires a strong boat edge, resulting in a weighted paddle. The length of the backwash is a factor in evaluating a side-surfing hole's strength. The longer, the stronger—and the more dangerous.

The best side surfing is done with the boat edged and the head and body balanced over the boat (figure 8.8). Unfortunately, many paddlers instinctively place the paddle far away from the boat for outrigger-type support. The flaw to this approach is that the blade keeps sinking. The more the blade reaches from the boat, the more the head and shoulders move off-center, and the more paddle pressure is needed to stay upright.

Figure 8.7 An ender.

Figure 8.8 Side surfing.

Simply find a balance point where pressure on the blade is unnecessary. Use the blade to move you across and back through the hole. Use just enough edge to keep the boat from flipping upstream. Stay loose in the hips for the ride. Tight muscles tire quickly, and balance is lost. Don't allow tension inside your boat. Your body should feel relaxed and balanced over the boat. Remember to breathe!

For safety, hold your arms low, elbows well below the shoulders and in front of your torso. Shoulder dislocations are infrequent but the most common injury in kayaking. They happen during extended arm positions. During torso rotation, your elbows should remain in front of your shoulders and close to your body. Be especially careful to avoid upstream braces in shallow holes. Instead, tuck your head tight to the cockpit as you flip. If you feel stuck trying to move the paddle around while side surfing, you are probably leaning out over the water, stiff, like a bell buoy. Instead, move the blade closer to the boat to center your weight and J-lean.

For balance purposes, use only gentle pressure on the paddle. Also try moving forward and backward in the hole or turn the angle of the blade to a 40-degree angle to move you laterally one direction and then 45-degrees in the other direction to move you back again. Use the blade in high-brace or low-brace positions.

Paddlers' River Hazards

The following river hazards force paddlers to adopt an inquisitive attitude. The river sense of experienced boaters is based on this approach.

Don't let these descriptions intimidate you. Your purpose is to understand the hazards clearly, enabling you to know when they are a factor in your safety.

Foot Entrapment

A foot entrapment is simply catching a foot in rocks on the bottom of the river. If your foot becomes caught in deep, fast water, the force of the water moving by you can pin you to the river's bottom, unable to free your foot or surface for much-needed air. Foot entrapment is caused by trying to stand up while getting swept downstream, usually in water midthigh to midtorso deep. Prevention is easy: Stay in the safe swimmer's position (on your back, feet up and pointed downstream) unless the water is less than knee deep. A good rule of thumb is to maintain the swimmer's self-rescue position until you are in water that is too shallow to swim in, then you can stand and walk out.

Part of the skill practice you will receive with a certified whitewater instructor may involve aggressively swimming and maneuvering through rapids, on your back, looking downriver and your feet pointed at the side of the river you wish to avoid. In very deep water, practice swimming freestyle, on your belly. River-swimming wisdom is to ball up when swimming over a sheer drop of more than 3 feet (.9 meters).

Strainers

Strainers are trees or single branches in the current, with river water flowing through, causing a severe pinning hazard. Strainers are caused by erosion. Trees fall because of old age, floods, and storms. Look for them on wooded riverbanks and along small creeks after high water. They are often found on the outside of bends and on less-frequented rivers. Assume strainers are present unless you know otherwise. Use downstream vision to spot bobbing twigs or irregular flow patterns.

Human-Made Entrapments

Anything in the river made by humans is a constant cause of alarm and is inherently more dangerous than most things natural. Keep an eye out for bridge pilings; low-head dams; junked cars; and any human-made junk found commonly in urban riverways, under highway crossings, and at abandoned dam sites. Maintain a habit of visually scanning downstream. Avoid anything suspicious!

Broaches

Broaching is getting pinned on a rock, either amidships (near the center) or at the ends. Avoid sharp rocks that can potentially crease a boat or serve as a point to be wrapped by your kayak. Develop the instinct to lean into the rock, with your boat and body leaning together like a bell buoy. Reach your body out to "love the rock" (see chapter 5, page 91). Practice this skill with an instructor on gentle, shallow water until it becomes instinct. Although counterintuitive, leaning into the rock presents the boat hull to the oncoming current, allowing the water to pile and flow under the bottom of the boat. In some broach situations, the water piling under the boat (or pillowing under the boat) provides enough lift to float the paddler and boat over the problematic rock.

Undercut Rocks

Undercuts are a water feature where a slab of rock, or rock shape, forces the current flow to go under the surface. Learn to spot them by the dark shadow on the upstream side of the rock, the lack of pillowing action (water piling on the upstream side of the rock) by oncoming water, and the lack of a predictable eddy on the downstream side. Most dangerous undercuts are well known by locals and listed in guidebooks. Undercut rocks pose a serious threat to the paddler if approached on the upstream side. The paddler can become flushed under the rock with no clear certainty of clearing the undercut to be freed on the other side.

Entanglement

Never tie yourself, any pet, or any other person to a boat in moving water. If capsized, the paddler is better floating free from the boat and paddle. Dangling ropes may become wedged between rocks or downed trees, where the force of the water may make it nearly impossible to free a person who is tied or entangled. Getting tangled exiting your boat is most likely to be caused by ropes and loose lines in your boat. Practice wet exits, and critically evaluate your outfitting for entanglement potential. Treat throw ropes strung across the river as a potential hazard. Keep them neatly bagged, and carry a knife in your life jacket to cut problem lines.

Vertical Pins

Vertical pins occur when the bow buries and gets pinned on the bottom after a steep drop. This becomes a significant concern when you are paddling drops of more than 3 feet (.9 meters); the bow may be buried deeper that the cockpit

The song of the river ends not at her banks, but in the hearts of those who have loved her.

Buffalo Joe

PADDLING TIP

You should be comfortable swimming any rapid you paddle because sooner or later you may actually swim it. Come out of your boat and take a rescue course. Learn how to actually swim whitewater. . . and increase your comfort.

height of the paddler, resulting in the paddler's being trapped underwater. Paddling a boat with a large-volume bow reduces this risk substantially. That's why boats marketed as "creek boats" have high volume in the bows.

Hydraulics

A hydraulic results when water flows over a ledge, rock outcropping, or other rock feature, allowing water to drop and form a depression downstream. Water rushes from downstream to fill in the depression, resulting in a lateral whirlpool action. Hydraulics are found all over whitewater rivers. Most are fun and challenging. Some are deadly killers because, once trapped in the backwash, it is difficult to escape. The killer hydraulics have evenly formed backwash, with water moving back upstream for at least 4 feet (1.2 meters), holding the boat and paddler with incredible force. Holes with more of a wave shape are intimidating but typically less hazardous than water flowing smoothly upstream. Hydraulics are found below many human-made low-head dams. Dams and natural hydraulics below ledges that are very regular, and perpendicular to the current, are far more dangerous than hydraulics angled with one end downstream.

Long Swims

Many people unfamiliar with the sport might expect long swims to be a primary killer. Since most beginner and intermediate rivers have long, flat pools of slow-moving water between the drops, this is rarely the case. Wearing a tight life jacket, matching your ability to an appropriate river, and being dressed for a swim can be excellent defense against a long swim. Of course another great precaution is a competent group of friends with either a shore- or boat-based rescue plan.

Dealing With Fear

Fear of whitewater is caused like any fear: Confusion and a lack of specific understanding allow your mind to manufacture anxiety, ill ease, and fear emotions. Specifically identifying the risks and choosing exactly where you paddle will go a long way toward harnessing your fears. Very few hazards are lurking in every rapid. Knowing when not to worry will undoubtedly make most of the sport more pleasant.

A common way to aggravate fears is by paddling with groups whose experience and thrill interests differ from yours. Choose your paddling companions carefully, and paddle with people of similar skills and interests. The purpose is to challenge yourself while having fun.

To deal with your river fears, remember that fear is a deeply ingrained protective mechanism. The horrible feelings you get are nothing more than extra energy for doing battle. Instead of thinking of yourself as nervous, think of having extra energy. Treat your mind to rerun images of making rapids successfully rather than dwelling on the worst that can happen.

Your vision patterns will match the water difficulty you paddle. Beginners tend to look only at the bow and slightly ahead. Intermediates tend to see eddies along the shore and look well down the rapid. Expert paddlers catch eddies while scanning downstream for hazards and upstream for other boaters. Developing your vision patterns will actually improve your skill level.

PREVENTABLE RISKS IN WHITEWATER BOATING

Attitude plays a huge role in successful paddling. Kent Ford, ACA instructor trainer educator and world-champion paddler, recounts this story about the role of a paddler's mind-set:

On the first day of a beginner course, I remember standing thigh deep in Lake Fontana, gazing off at the southern tip of the Smoky Mountains, waiting patiently for the last student in my kayak class to paddle over for rolling instruction. The extra time it took him to drift to me provided clues to his fears. And, as I had guessed, he panicked when he finally let his boat flip upside down. "How do you feel?" I queried. "Okay," he muttered. "What's on your mind?" I asked. "Drowning," he admitted.

Gulp. As a professional instructor, I believe in insulating my students from unnecessary worry by teaching skills in a logical, reassuring progression. An outline of the day's activities, closely supervised wet exits, and maintaining a high regard for safety precautions usually serves this purpose. Unfortunately, this whitewater-bound beginner had arrived with fearful misconceptions about safety in the sport. His well-meaning friends had sent him off with intimidating comments about his poor, ownerless dog starving. They had made teasing claims to his posthumous bank account. Then, after signing the purposefully graphic course waiver, my student's insecurities had toppled.

"Are you afraid of drowning here on the lake?" I asked. "No," he swallowed. "On the river then?" I pursued. "Well ...," he paused. "How many of the 150,000 people who travel the Nantahala each year do you think drown?" I asked, imagining my student's mind racing into the double digits. "Two drownings in 20 years," I explained. "Neither was a kayaker. One wasn't wearing a life jacket."

Immediately following this incident I described to the whole class the five preventable causes of death that give whitewater sports a risky reputation.

"Number one, alcohol is a common cause of accidents. That is clearly not an issue for us today. Number two, not wearing a tight-fitting PFD. Our class has already discussed this topic. Number three, no prior education in the sport causes 95 percent of whitewater accidents. Here we are in class, avoiding that mistake. Number four, flooded rivers are a frequent killer. Sadly, we are in the midst of a five-year drought. Although we would welcome higher water, floods are certainly not a risk to us today. Number five, hypothermia. Clearly I am in the greatest danger, shivering slightly from three hours of roll instructing. You, however, are in no risk, basking in 90-degree Fahrenheit [32 degree Celsius] temperatures with a wet suit available."

I noticed everyone's shoulders relax as I reviewed whitewater sports' five unnecessary killers. The class closed with smiles on everyone's face.

Trip Planning and River Sense

Chapter 4 presents a number of elements of trip planning. Following these trip-planning concepts helps the paddler develop a sense of the river to be traveled. River sense is honed through experience, but it begins with a healthy respect for information from printed, electronic, and living sources. Before starting the trip, consult maps, guidebooks, and people knowledgeable about the river. Maps reveal much about the river including the average gradient, dams or other obstructions, and access points for emergencies and rescue.

Guidebooks usually give a detailed account of the river along with shuttle information. Always check when the guidebook was published. A major flood can totally change a guidebook's account of the river, making some rapids more difficult and others easier. Check with knowledgeable people such as conservation officers, members of local paddling clubs, or outfitters who are familiar with the river on a daily basis.

Be sure to check the stream flow or the river gauge before embarking on the trip. The U.S. Geological Survey (USGS) provides real-time online stream-gauge readings for thousands of streams in the United States. Stream volumes can change quickly after a summer thunderstorm or an unseen event upstream, so always be prepared for rising levels and the characteristics of water as it changes depth and force.

Before the Trip

Planning a river trip involves more than just river skills. A bit of research will ensure that you are prepared to comply with all local, state, and federal laws. These laws may include launch permits or fees, state boat registration requirements, and zoning regulations of certain waterways. Check with local authorities before launching your boat.

Plan a trip no longer than a half day for your first river outing. A short trip covering 2 to 3 miles (3 to 5 kilometers) gives you a chance to hone skills and river maneuvers without the worry of being on the water too long. A trip of modest length also provides a good opportunity to check equipment and train muscles new to the sport.

At the Site

The paddlers' shuttle is an activity that precedes most downriver trips. This is when the group plans and places a vehicle (or vehicles) at a designated take-out downstream. Paddling trips do not always end at the spot where you started. On rivers and lakes, traveling from point A to point B is part of the fun of exploration. Watching participants new to the sport sort out how to execute a shuttle can be comical. Many a paddler has ended up at the take-out having left the car keys in a vehicle at the put-in!

Here are foolproof steps for setting up a shuttle:

1. Travel to the put-in, and drop off kayaks and all gear needed on the river. Remember the essentials: boat, paddle, life jacket, protective gear, and food and water.
2. Participants drive all vehicles to the take-out. Some group members should stay with the gear for safety and security.
3. Leave all vehicles except those needed for the return. Be sure to leave dry clothes in vehicles at the take-out. Remember to take your vehicle keys.
4. Drive back to the put-in in as few vehicles as possible (don't overload, and use your seat belts).
5. Pack your vehicle keys in a secure place at the put-in (of course, carry with you the keys for the vehicles at the take-out).
6. Paddle and enjoy the trip.
7. Take out and load all kayaks.
8. Travel back to the put-in.
9. Pick up vehicles left at the put-in. Transfer kayaks if needed, or return to the take-out to pick up the remaining boats.
10. Travel home.

During the Trip

When on the water, the lead generally is the person most familiar with the lake or river. The sweep boat carries first aid and safety gear and should carry one of the most highly skilled and experienced paddlers on the outing. All remaining boats stay between the lead and sweep boats. On a river, it is expected that a paddler will never lose sight of the boat following. If that boat goes out of sight, the paddler should pull over and wait. Likewise, the boat ahead should pull over and wait, and so on throughout the group.

The sweep boat assists any paddlers needing assistance. On a regular basis, the lead boat should pull over to rest, allowing the remaining paddlers including the sweep to catch up to assess the trip. These rest periods are vital for keeping spirits high and making sure participants drink water, eat high-energy foods, and are not suffering from environmental conditions.

Vision, Scouting, and Decision Making

A paddler must learn to look downstream. This sounds like common sense, but often novice paddlers focus on what is happening immediately under them. This paddler "tunnel vision" causes mishaps that can be avoided. With practice, a paddler raises his or her vision and starts looking downstream or in front of him or her. Be aware of the need to constantly look downstream.

Two rules of thumb for running rivers:

1. Never paddle anything you would not want to swim.
2. When in doubt, get out and scout.

Scouting involves beaching the boat above a drop, and once all paddlers are safely ashore, walking down to look at a drop and plan a route (figure 8.9). This is a decision opportunity for each paddler in the group. After viewing the drop, each person can choose to run it or walk it. A paddler deciding

Figure 8.9 Get out, scout the river, and plan your route before a big rapid.

to walk a drop should be congratulated for his personal decision and not scoffed or laughed at. Group support is highly valued, and it is up to each individual to determine if he feels up to running a drop and risking a swim or other mishap. If paddlers choose to run a drop, often the group will set safety lines or position themselves with appropriate safety gear at the bottom to assist if needed.

Carry a throw rope when scouting. Also, make sure everyone keeps their life jackets on and zipped while scouting a drop. River banks can be slippery, and many a person has taken a swim while scouting.

Once in a good position to see the entire drop, determine where you want to end up at the bottom of the rapid (hopefully upright, of course!). After determining your desired end point, look carefully at the river current to determine how you will get there. Often a combination of catching eddies, peelouts, ferries, or other maneuvers are needed to get you where you want to go, all while avoiding holes and other hazards (figure 8.10). Combinations of river maneuvers such as this are river running at its best. By practicing paddling maneuvers in less-risky conditions, you gain the confidence and skills needed to perform them when they count the most.

Figure 8.10   You can also scout the river while in an eddy.

Summary

The key to safe whitewater paddling is developing a healthy respect for the river with good preparation for the outing both physically and mentally. River-reading skills provide the visual guide for safe passage. The key to reading water is to lift your vision! Don't just look at your bow. Look where you want to go and at what lies in between. Look for visible rocks, water features formed by rocks under the surface, and hazards. As you scan the rapid, look far downstream to figure out where the current ends. You might see some rocks above the water deflecting the current. Figuring out why the current was deflected is the key to reading the rapid.

An instructor can help you learn to identify river hazards, such as undercut rocks or bridge pilings. Tree branches forming strainers are one of the most dangerous hazards in the sport. Development of your river sense will result in scanning for bouncing twigs and unexplained currents that might indicate a strainer. Learn to identify potential danger spots, then concentrate your vision on where you want to go rather than at what you want to avoid.

Learning to read water takes time and practice, so paddle within your ability and experience, and don't just follow other boaters. Instead, explore easy and safe rapids by picking your own line.

Leader's Preparedness and Responsibility

☐ Know the river or lake to be paddled. Guide booklets and topography maps are valuable references in trip planning. Have knowledge of the difficult parts of the trip including rapids, open water crossings, and low-head dams. Be aware of wind and river levels. Plan alternatives in case conditions are too windy, too high, or too low.

☐ Set up locations for the put-in and take-out along with a possible lunch break stop. Consider time and distance. It is better to plan too short a trip than too long. Arrange for the vehicle shuttle. Consider leaving a shuttle vehicle at the half-way point in case you decide to take-out early.

☐ Limit the size of the group to a number you can comfortably control. Designated group leaders should be experienced paddlers. Decisions on the participation of inexperienced boaters should be based on total group strength. Remember, the welfare of the group is the major responsibility, and a balance of experienced paddlers with the less experienced will make for a more-enjoyable trip for all.

☐ Plan so that all necessary group equipment is present on the trip.

☐ If the trip is into a wilderness area, or for an extended period, plans should be filed with appropriate authorities or left with someone who will contact them after a certain time. The establishment of a late-return phone number can save time and worry for everyone involved.

Participant's Preparedness and Responsibility

☐ Be a competent swimmer, with the ability to handle yourself underwater. If you are not a strong swimmer, you must have water confidence to ensure you do not panic if involved in a capsize. Swimming in a river is not the same as swimming in a swimming pool.

☐ Wear a properly fitting life jacket when on or around the water.

☐ Be suitably equipped.

☐ Keep your craft under control. Control must be good enough at all times to stop or reach shore before reaching any danger. Know your boating ability. Do not enter a rapid unless reasonably sure you can safely navigate it or swim the entire rapid in the event of a capsizing.

☐ Be sure to keep an appropriate distance between kayaks. This distance may vary based on conditions. Keep the kayak behind you in sight. Never get ahead of the assigned lead boat or behind the assigned sweep boat. Both lead and sweep positions should be held by experienced paddlers with knowledge of the water being traveled.

☐ Keep a lookout for hazards, and avoid them.

☐ Respect the rights of anglers, private property owners, and others. Be courteous.

CHAPTER 9

Pursuing Paddlesports: Pass It On

Humankind has not woven the web of life. We are but one thread within it. Whatever we do to the web, we do to ourselves. All things are bound together. All things connect.

Chief Seattle

The opportunities to explore the world by kayak are as varied as the landscape itself. From sea kayak adventures from Alaska to Florida, whitewater extreme rodeos in the Rockies, and short outings with a local livery or outfitter, nearly every part of the globe has paddling options for your enjoyment.

Use and Stewardship of Resources

The paddling lifestyle is not one that we should take for granted. Each day, access to our nation's water resources are being purchased, developed by private developers, and locked up to the common adventurer who does not own a part of the access. Paddling clubs and conservation and stewardship organizations work hard to ensure the general paddling public retains rights to access our precious waterways. We as paddlers must continue to do our part to care for and protect our waterways for our children and future generations.

Paddlesports are accessible to persons of all abilities, all races, all income levels. You must only have the desire and seek a mentor, instructor, or guide to expose you to the possibilities. If you have experience, plan to be a mentor to those who have not shared in the world of rivers, lakes, estuaries, ponds, and tidal areas. Paddling clubs exist around the United States and Canada and are a perfect way to meet new friends, connect with experienced people willing to share knowledge, and find a social network of paddling partners.

Many paddlers are so totally committed to the paddling lifestyle that it would be hard to imagine what they would do if they could not pursue the sport and think, plan, and dream about it. A number of groups work in direct support of the shared water resource and are worthy of support:

American Rivers is a national river conservation network that protects our water resources. Each year it announces the nation's most endangered rivers. See the list at www.americanrivers.org, and support river protection in your state and community.

American Whitewater works to ensure whitewater runs are available for recreation use. Support its work by visiting www.americanwhitewater.org.

Environmental Impact

The Leave No Trace doctrine covers much in the area of environmental impact, and although most is common sense, some is not intuitive and requires education on how what we do affects the environment. Users of the outdoors can and should be the stewards of the outdoors. Every small slide that cuts a rut in a riverbank will cause erosion of that bank. No piece of plastic will disappear on its own in a lifetime; all trash in our waterways detracts from the health and beauty of our environment.

Social Impacts

Aside from environmental impact, kayaking continues to have an impact on society. In recent years, it has been listed as the fastest-growing outdoor activity, and it continues to grow because of the diversity of craft and the people who buy them. The percentage of people who use paddlecraft for the thrill of running whitewater and ocean surfing seems to remain fairly static, but the number of recreational paddlers who seek a life sport that provides healthy outdoor exercise grows geometrically. More and more advertisements for all sorts of goods and services have paddlecraft prominently displayed.

Paddling is a part of our culture and that of many nations and races. There are generic paddling clubs as well as special clubs and organizations, including a number of international ones. Instructors from other countries often come to the United States to teach and learn and vice versa. There are women-only groups, groups for persons with disabilities, historical paddling groups, geographic groups, and more. All provide opportunities for social interaction. Most people paddle with groups of friends and make new ones by paddling.

Paddling draws positive attention to what our environment is and what it can and should be—healthy air and water to enjoy exercise and a wonderful outdoor life sport. Nothing could be better. Unfortunately, the younger generation today has a greater number of opportunities to be introduced to new computer games than to paddle a kayak.

Kayaking can be a family sport. Children should be at least 7 before they go on their own in a boat, and it should be a very controlled experience to avoid any chance of incidents that could turn them off forever. Kids 10 to 15 can really thrive in the sport and learn it very quickly. As with any activity, though, kids have less sense of responsibility and overall safety. Very young children can go on short sea kayaking tours in a tandem boat, especially when the trip is in a protected area with easy exit options.

Limitations of Use

On some rivers, the paddler must first obtain a user permit. Permit systems regulate the number of paddlers who can access the waterway on any given date or time. Recreational demand and use patterns are constantly changing, and allocation systems must accurately adjust to such changes. Historic use patterns on use-limited rivers may not accurately reflect the actual level of demand generated by all user groups.

Decisions to limit access and use of the nation's waterways should never be taken lightly. The American Canoe Association (ACA) recognizes that on some waterways the public demand for use is greater than the resource can accommodate without degrading the resource and compromising recreational experiences. The number of people participating in canoeing, kayaking, and rafting has increased substantially in recent years. All individuals seeking to explore waterways by canoe, kayak, or raft should have equal opportunities for access. The safe, responsible, and ethical use of the nation's rivers is a shared concern of resource management agencies and the greater paddlesport community.

Paddlers who have developed the necessary skills to safely and responsibly explore wild, remote, or challenging waterways on their own have invested time, effort, and money to be able to enjoy self-reliant outdoor experiences. Commercial outfitters have likewise invested time, effort, and money to provide paddlers with valuable services that enable them to safely experience the nation's wild, remote, or otherwise challenging waterways. Liveries and outfitters can be viewed as the community's gatekeepers, introducing the vast majority of entry-level paddlers to paddlesports on local and less-challenging waters.

Semipublic and educational groups such as clubs, camps, and institutional programs have not always enjoyed equal access to the nation's use-limited waterways. Agencies managing use-limited rivers have often allocated use without the benefit of a reliable demand study or other scientific information. It is imperative that the paddling community be involved on a local level with issues regarding waterway access in order to ensure paddling opportunities into the future.

Paddler Environmental Ethics

Paddlers are responsible for the resource and should provide role models of good, ethical behavior (see figure 9.1). Leave No Trace is an organization that has developed and teaches outdoor ethics for river corridors. The following principles for paddlers are based on the framework of Leave No Trace's message:

1. Never litter; always pack out trash.
   - Carry a bag or container specifically for trash removal.
   - Secure trash in your boat so it will withstand wind or capsize.
2. Conduct all toilet activity at least 200 feet (60 meters) from any water body.

Figure 9.1 Practicing environmental ethics is every paddler's responsibility.

- All solid human waste must be buried 4 to 8 inches (10 to 20 centimeters) deep or packed out.
- Used toilet paper or sanitary napkins should be packed out. In wet conditions, where no wildfire hazard exists, toilet paper may also be burned in the hole with waste (cat hole) before filling in the hole with dirt.
- Urinating directly in the water may be advisable on certain desert waterways or at sea. Consult Leave No Trace (www.lnt.org) for specific guidelines.
- Never dispose of any foodstuff in the same location as human waste, since it will prompt animals to dig up the waste.
- Check with the local resource manager for location-specific guidance.
- Exact procedures vary depending on the specific environmental characteristics (climate, soil, and so on) of your paddling or camping location. Consult Leave No Trace (www.lnt.org) for specific guidelines.

3. Pack out human waste in sensitive or heavily used environments.
   - Raft-supported trips should carry portable toilet systems designed for river use.
   - Portable toilet systems should be compatible with locally available dump stations.
   - Paddlers on canoe- or kayak-only trips can carry specially designed disposable bags to facilitate packing out solid waste (such as the Wag Bag from Phillips Environmental Products).

4. Do not disturb wildlife.
   - Observe wildlife quietly from a distance.
   - Utilize binoculars or telephoto camera lenses to obtain closer views.
   - Maintain 50 to 100 yards (45 to 90 meters) between you and marine mammals.
   - Never attempt to feed wildlife.
   - Never leave food or trash accessible to wildlife.
   - On multiday paddling trips in bear country, store food and trash in specially designed bear-resistant bags or canisters.
   - Watch for and avoid any wildlife dens and nesting or spawning areas.
   - Never allow your craft to drift into wading or swimming wildlife.

5. Minimize impacts to shore when launching, portaging, scouting, or taking out.
   - Do not drag boats on the ground when launching or taking out.
   - Launch or take out boats on sandy beaches or rocky areas.

- Avoid disturbing (marring) soft ground, especially on sloping terrain such as riverbanks.
- Try to avoid stepping on vegetation.

6. Avoid building campfires, except in officially established fire rings or for emergencies.
   - For overnight trips, use a camping stove for cooking.
   - If you must build a fire, utilize established fire rings if available.
   - Obey all resource management agency guidelines and regulations regarding campfires.
   - Thoroughly douse campfires with water, and verify they are completely extinguished before leaving unattended.
   - Scatter ashes, and return any disturbed terrain features to their original condition.

7. Consult the Leave No Trace Web site (www.lnt.org) and local resource managers for additional guidance.

Reprinted, by permission, from the American Canoe Association.

Paddler Etiquette and Standards of Conduct

Kayak etiquette is no more or less than good manners while paddling as well as common sense about respecting other people and the environment itself. You wait your turn, and when it is your turn, you are mindful that others are waiting. On whitewater rivers, the eddies may be large enough for only one or two boats, so hanging out in one of these eddies may take away opportunity and perhaps even the safety of another paddler. Don't pull in front of another paddler, and be aware that the most skilled have much better control of their craft than the inexperienced. Paddle defensively, stay within your limits, and give up the right of way to stay in control.

The paddling community shares a common standard of conduct. Observing these commonsense principles will show others you are serious about your sport.

1. Obey all rules and regulations.
   - Be informed about all applicable rules and regulations before launching your vessel (see figure 9.2).
   - When paddling on multiple-use waterways, know the generally accepted rules of navigation (boating's "rules of the road").
   - Avoid paddling near areas of heightened security, such as military bases and nuclear power plants.

2. Respect private property. Use only public lands and access points.
   - Do not cross or occupy private property without permission from the owner.

Figure 9.2 Paddlers should learn the applicable rules and regulations of their venue before launching their kayaks.

- When utilizing private property with permission, never litter or engage in any behavior likely to upset the landowner.
- Help landowners police and maintain access areas they make available for public use.
- Be informed about the navigability status of the waterway and what constitutes the high-water mark.
3. Be considerate to others on the water.
- Paddle in control, and avoid drifting into others.
- Avoid interfering with the recreational activities of others.
- Be courteous and polite when communicating with others.
- Never engage in lewd or inappropriate behavior.
- When playing in hydraulic river features such as waves or holes, whitewater paddlers should yield the right of way to boats traveling downstream.
4. Give fishers a wide berth.
- Pay attention to the location of fishers and of their fishing lines.
- Avoid passing within the casting range of fishers whenever possible.
- If you must pass within casting range, time passage to when the fisher has reeled in the line.
- Pass by anglers as quickly and as quietly as practicable.

5. Never change clothes in public view.

 ⊕ Utilize available changing facilities or restrooms.

 ⊕ When no changing facility is available, utilize vehicles, tents, changing apparel, or landscape features to change clothes beyond the view of others.

6. Respect local culture and standards of conduct.

 ⊕ Respect local community standards of decency.

 ⊕ Always assume others may be offended by public nudity.

 ⊕ Avoid using offensive language.

 ⊕ Enrich your experience by learning about the heritage and culture of the places you paddle.

 ⊕ Support local businesses with your patronage whenever practicable.

7. Give back to the waterway.

 ⊕ Volunteer for organized waterway cleanups and improvement projects (figure 9.3).

 ⊕ Report pollution or other waterway degradation to appropriate officials and the ACA.

 ⊕ Support causes and organizations that are working to safeguard the nation's recreational waters.

Reprinted, by permission, from the American Canoe Association.

Figure 9.3 Participating in river clean-up days allows you to give back to the waterway.

Paddling Opportunities

The opportunities to explore the world by kayak are as varied as the landscape itself. In most regions, local outfitters offer classes or tours that are a good way to get introduced to the waterways of the area. You can learn about the difficulty and specific hazards of various local trips. Talk to the local paddlers to get their recommendations on where to learn more.

AMERICAN CANOE ASSOCIATION

The American Canoe Association (ACA) is a nationwide not-for-profit organization that serves the broader paddling public by providing education on matters related to paddling, by supporting stewardship of the paddling environment, and by enabling programs and events to support paddlesport recreation. The ACA is uniquely qualified to help individuals and organizations understand how paddlesports can contribute to quality of life through enabling safe and positive paddling experiences. It is the objective of the ACA to be the recognized primary resource for individuals, organizations, agencies, and regulators for information and guidance on all aspects of paddling. For complete information, visit the ACA Web site at www.americancanoe.org.

The ACA's strategic tenets are education, stewardship, and recreation.

1. **Paddlesport education.** ACA has long been a leader in the area of paddlesport education, promoting "gateway" paddling education to reach the broader public as well as mastery-level programs for the paddlesport enthusiast. ACA's certified instructors and trainers are the gold standard in the paddlesport industry.

2. **Stewardship.** The ACA is a recognized leader of conservation and stewardship efforts on behalf of paddlers. The ACA maintains and enhances both the natural and regulatory environments for paddlers at the national level.

3. **Recreation.** Since its inception in 1880, the ACA has been actively involved in paddling recreation, events, and competition. Serving all segments of the paddling public, the ACA promotes the activity of paddling, including the activity itself, its value, and its healthy benefits.

Paddling With Clubs

There are strong networks of paddling clubs across the United States and Canada. Many of the best are ACA Paddle America clubs or ACA affiliate clubs. For a list of paddling clubs in your area, visit www.americancanoe.org/Recreation/clubs.lasso.

Paddling With an Outfitter

The Paddlesports Industry Association (PIA) is the premier trade association promoting paddlesports. The PIA serves the paddlesport industry, including canoe, kayak, and raft rentals, retailers, liveries, outfitters, manufacturers, and distributors. PIA members help outdoor enthusiasts experience the fun and joy of rafting, canoeing, and kayaking the lakes, rivers, whitewaters, streams, creeks, bays, and coastal waters in the United States and internationally.

PIA members are some of the most experienced outfitters in the world. Rent kayaks in the Ozark Mountains of Missouri or buy a recreational kayak to bird-watch in your local stream. Run whitewater rafts down the Ocoee or buy a "new school" play boat from the best whitewater experts in the United States. For an outfitter in your area, visit www.paddlesportsindustry.org.

Summary

People paddle for a number of reasons. We kayak for relaxation, to be close to nature, to be with friends and family. We kayak for the camaraderie, the fellowship, the adrenaline, the togetherness brought about through being on the water. There is another level of deep satisfaction that can be attained . . . the satisfaction of passing the enjoyment of paddlesports on to others.

Somewhere around you, there is a kid who is waiting to be introduced to paddlesports and a neighbor who is looking for a way to spend more time with his family. Make a resolution to share your interest of paddling with someone new. Become a mentor, and pass the passion of paddling on.

As paddlers, we are just one group of the minority users of our waterways. Outdoor ethics should be an accepted code of how and what things are done, or not done, in the outdoors.

Resource stewardship (caring for and protecting the waterways) is a by-product of awareness. Awareness is developed to a large degree by experience with the resource. There is little that gives more experience with the resource than paddling.

To ensure that recreational paddling shares a future in our society, present-day enthusiasts should care enough to pass the legacy of these lifetime pursuits on to the next generation. We each have a role to play in investing in the future of paddlesports. It is up to each of us to pass it on.

Web Resources

International Paddling Organizations

American Canoe Association (ACA)
www.americancanoe.org
The primary resource for individuals, organizations, agencies, and regulators for information and guidance on all aspects of paddling. Click on Water Trails for a list of hundreds of water trails across North America.

Asian Canoe Confederation
www.canoeacc.com

Australian Canoeing
www.canoe.org.au
This site offers paddling education, competition, clubs, paddling in Australia, and international paddling trips.

British Canoe Union
www.bcu.org.uk
This site includes links to paddling clubs in England, Northern Ireland, Scotland, and Wales.

Confederation of African Canoeing
www.kayakafrica.org

European Canoe Association
www.canoe-europe.org

International Canoe Federation
www.canoeicf.com/default.asp
The International Canoe Federation is the world governing body of paddlesports, including Olympic and world championship kayaking.

New Zealand Recreational Canoeing Association
www.rivers.org.nz

Paddle Canada
http://paddlingcanada.com/main.php

Fitness

GreatOutdoors.com
www.greatoutdoors.com/published/healthfitness
Lots of articles about outdoor-related fitness. There is also a section for paddling-specific health and fitness articles.

Men's Health
www.menshealth.com
Catering to men, this Web site offers free videos; tips for getting started, and lots of ways to change, enhance, or improve your workout.

MyPyramid.gov
www.mypyramid.gov

Whole Fitness
www.wholefitness.com
Offers a good overall summary of exercises, stretches, and diet tips for those looking to learn more about physical fitness.

Women's Health
www.womenshealthmag.com
This is the women's version of the Men's Health site, focusing on women-specific issues relating to fitness and health.

General Interest

America Outdoors
www.americaoutdoors.org

American Rivers
www.americanrivers.org/site/PageServer

American Whitewater
www.americanwhitewater.org

Boundary Waters Canoe Area Wilderness
www.bwcaw.org

Canoe and Kayak Product Reviews
www.paddling.net/Reviews
Visit this rating system of boat reviews by paddlers for paddlers.

Hypothermia Prevention, Recognition and Treatment
www.hypothermia.org
This site outlines the recommended treatment of hypothermia in the field.

National Association of State Boating Law Administrators
www.nasbla.org

National Safe Boating Council
www.safeboatingcouncil.org

Paddler Magazine.com
http://paddlermagazine.com/advertisers.shtml#KAY
Visit this link at Paddler Magazine.com for a list of boat manufacturers, paddles, gear, clothing, and links to manufacturer Web sites.

Paddlesports Industry Association
www.paddlesportsindustry.com

Performance Video
www.performancevideo.com
This site offers some of the finest paddlesport instructional videos available.

USA Canoe/Kayak
www.usack.org

Governmental Agencies

Bureau of Land Management
www.blm.gov/wo/st/en.html

Department of the Interior
www.doi.gov

National Park Service
www.nps.gov

NOAA Weather
www.nws.noaa.gov

Recreation.Gov
www.recreation.gov

United States Coast Guard Auxiliary
www.cgaux.org

United States Coast Guard Office of Boating Safety
www.uscgboating.org

U.S. Forest Service
www.fs.fed.us

USCG Stream Gauges
http://waterdata.usgs.gov/nwis/rt

Success Checks

Chapter 1

1. Kayaking originated in the early 1950s as a means of paddlesport recreation.
    a. true
    b. false

2. Kayaking is a high-impact activity for the upper body.
    a. true
    b. false

3. Kayaking can contribute to your overall well-being, mentally and physically.
    a. true
    b. false

4. Nearly every water venue is suitable for kayaking.
    a. true
    b. false

5. The best resource for finding information on where to paddle locally is through the Internet.
    a. true
    b. false

6. Maps and charts show every known human-made or natural hazard.
    a. true
    b. false

7. Rivers and creeks are subject to change as water levels rise and fall with change of season and weather patterns.
    a. true
    b. false

8. When deciding to become a kayaker, you must first consider your interests, such as river, flatwater, or coastal paddling.
    a. true
    b. false

Chapter 2

1. Being physically fit enables you to better take care of yourself on the water.

    a. true

    b. false

2. Physical exhaustion has no impact on your ability to think clearly.

    a. true

    b. false

3. Stronger, more muscular kayakers are better kayakers because they have more power.

    a. true

    b. false

4. A paddler who is flexible is less likely to be injured than a paddler who is stiff and cannot easily adapt to a variety of circumstances.

    a. true

    b. false

5. Cardiovascular fitness helps in all components of physical fitness.

    a. true

    b. false

6. Stretching should be done only on land because there is no way to stand on water.

    a. true

    b. false

7. You should drink just enough water so that your urine runs clear.

    a. true

    b. false

8. A good rule of thumb for determining caloric intake is that calories in should exceed calories out.

    a. true

    b. false

9. Competitive paddlers take training and nutrition very seriously.

    a. true

    b. false

10. Entering nonpaddling competitions, such as triathlons or bike races, is a great way to stay in shape and add variety to your workouts.

    a. true

    b. false

11. Which of the following is *not* a key component of physical fitness?
   a. strength
   b. flexibility
   c. energy
   d. endurance
   e. cardiovascular fitness

12. Listening to your body means
   a. knowing that even though it hurts, you should keep doing it
   b. putting your wrist to your ear and listening for a tiny, quiet voice
   c. being aware of how physical activity affects your body and knowing when to stop
   d. none of the above

13. Which of the following would be a good choice of food while kayaking:
   a. potato chips
   b. dried fruit
   c. ice cream
   d. granola bar
   e. b and d

14. Which of the following should you *not* do while stretching:
   a. take consistent, deep breaths
   b. bounce in order to touch your toes
   c. warm up to get the blood flowing
   d. hold your stretch for 10 to 15 seconds

15. Which of the following can be used to assist in stretching:
   a. tree
   b. paddle
   c. buddy
   d. all of the above

16. Which of the following is *not* a good example of a cardiovascular workout?
   a. swimming
   b. bicycling
   c. heavy lifting
   d. running

17. Push-ups engage which of the following muscle groups:
   a. chest
   b. triceps
   c. shoulders
   d. all of the above

18. Which of the following muscle groups relates to your body's "core":
    a. biceps
    b. calves
    c. abdominals
    d. shoulders

19. Which of the following is *not* a component of a quality training program?
    a. action
    b. quality
    c. variety
    d. fun
    e. none of the above

20. Which of the following is *not* a good resource for learning more about physical fitness?
    a. physician
    b. personal trainer
    c. Internet
    d. library
    e. none of the above—these are all great resources!

Chapter 3

1. A kayak designed for whitewater is typically longer than one designed for touring.
   a. true
   b. false

2. All other measurements being equal, a shorter and fatter boat will travel faster than a long, narrow, tippy boat.
   a. true
   b. false

3. When picking out a kayak, study the bow of the boat (where it enters the water). This entry point can help you determine a boat design that is fast versus one that can turn the quickest.
   a. true
   b. false

4. A boat that remains wide along its length will be more stable than one that widens briefly and then narrows again.
   a. true
   b. false

5. Width above the waterline is more an indication of stability than width below the waterline.
   a. true
   b. false

6. Secondary stability occurs when the kayaker tries rocking the boat from side to side and the boat feels very secure and stable.
   a. true
   b. false

7. Boats with hard chines have a lot of initial stability and generally very little secondary stability.
   a. true
   b. false

8. Rocker is the degree to which the hull curves from side to side.
   a. true
   b. false

9. Outfitting a kayak may include customized adjustments and modifications to seats, foot and thigh braces, and hip area.
   a. true
   b. false

10. When starting out, there is no real need to match the paddle to the paddler and the desired activity.
    a. true
    b. false

11. There is no need to use any special type of outdoor clothing when beginning to paddle.
    a. true
    b. false

12. It is important to reduce the risks of environmental problems such as hypothermia, dehydration, and sunburn.
    a. true
    b. false

13. A life jacket is also known as a personal flotation device, or PFD.
    a. true
    b. false

14. To size a paddle, hold it over you head with arms at right angles to the shaft. Touring paddles are generally longer than whitewater paddles.
    a. true
    b. false

15. To paddle, at minimum you need a paddle, boat, and life jacket. Add additional gear based on type of paddling and environmental conditions.

    a. true

    b. false

16. The ability to wet exit a kayak is critical if a spray skirt is worn.

    a. true

    b. false

17. Dress in layers based on the three Ws—wind, weather, and waves.

    a. true

    b. false

18. Cotton makes a good next-to-skin layer because it is very comfortable.

    a. true

    b. false

19. Helmets should be worn when paddling in fast-moving rivers or surf conditions.

    a. true

    b. false

Chapter 4

1. In some states, you may need to register your kayak or obtain a launch permit to use a waterway.

    a. true

    b. false

2. A kayaking outing should be geared to the strongest paddler.

    a. true

    b. false

3. One of the first steps in organizing a group outing is to inventory the skill level of the group.

    a. true

    b. false

4. As a trip leader, it is important to be familiar with a route before you take others along.

    a. true

    b. false

5. The difficulty of a well-planned trip can be altered by rain, strong winds, and heat.

   a. true

   b. false

6. Paddling guidebooks can be useful sources of information if they are up to date.

   a. true

   b. false

7. Even with Internet and published information about the water, it is wise to contact local guides or experts for up-to-date information.

   a. true

   b. false

8. A float plan informs others where you are going and when they should expect you to return.

   a. true

   b. false

9. Every paddler should carry personal gear and his share of group gear.

   a. true

   b. false

10. The sweep boat travels in front of the group to scan the waterway for hidden hazards.

    a. true

    b. false

11. If anyone in a paddling group has medical, physical, or emotional limitations, these should be shared with the trip leader and at least one other responsible person in the group.

    a. true

    b. false

12. A trip leader is responsible for herself and does not need to designate a qualified assistant who will act on her behalf in case of mishap.

    a. true

    b. false

13. The day of the trip is too late to cancel because of local conditions.

    a. true

    b. false

14. Each paddler is responsible for his or her own gear at the put-in, and the trip leaders can then relax and enjoy the outing.

    a. true

    b. false

15. Paddlers are responsible for knowing and following the navigation rules for waterways they paddle.

    a. true

    b. false

16. The law requires paddlers to display a light under certain conditions.

    a. true

    b. false

17. A kayaker has a right to safe passage and does not need to be concerned about anglers or swimmers in her path.

    a. true

    b. false

Chapter 5

1. If you do not have experience paddling in moving water, two very important things you should do before venturing out is to get training (take a class) and travel with someone who is experienced (go with a group that has paddled the river before).

    a. true

    b. false

2. Which of the following is a practical trick that can be used to help predict the weather:

    a. Know what jet vapor can tell you about the weather.

    b. Know what the various clouds or lack of them can tell you about the weather.

    c. Know what the color of the water can tell you about the weather.

    d. a and b

3. The 24-hour weather broadcast service is supplied by NOAA, the National Oceanic and Atmospheric Administration, which is a branch of the National Weather Service.

    a. true

    b. false

4. You cannot get into trouble with bad weather conditions when fair weather is forecast.

    a. true

    b. false

5. Rivers are dangerous to kayak because they have tremendous power, and they may be filled with hazards.

    a. true

    b. false

6. When a river turns, does water pile up on the outside or inside turn of the river's bend?

7. What is the name of the feature that is created behind an obstruction protruding from a fast-moving river?

8. The most common types of strainers that can cause serious problem in many rivers and should be avoided are
   a. fallen trees
   b. low-head dams
   c. bridge piers
   d. all of the above

9. If you capsize upstream of a strainer, you should make every effort to swim away from it. If you are going to be swept into the strainer, turn over on your belly and swim aggressively up and over it. Your life may depend on your getting yourself high enough onto the strainer.
   a. true
   b. false

10. A horizon line is the usual indicator of a riverwide obstacle commonly referred to as a
    a. pillow
    b. waterfall or low-head dam
    c. foot entrapment
    d. strainer

11. What is called the "drowning machine" because it is very efficient at drowning people should they get caught in one?
    a. a strainer
    b. a pot hole
    c. a low-head dam
    d. a bridge pier

12. You should never try to stand in fast-moving water that is above your knees or you could possibly experience a threatening situation referred to as
    a. drowning
    b. hypothermia
    c. pinning
    d. foot entrapment

13. Unless you are familiar with an area, you should avoid paddling and playing behind old human-made structures because they might contain reinforcing rods, sharp rocks, and other debris that could cause injury.
    a. true
    b. false

14. When a kayak is swept sideways into a rock or other obstruction, it is called a

   a. pin or broach

   b. capsize

   c. strainer

   d. drowning machine

15. The number one thing *any* paddler can do to stay safe on the water is to *always* wear his life jacket (personal flotation device, or PFD).

   a. true

   b. false

16. To prevent an unexpected plunge or capsizing into the water, what should you do?

   a. maintain three points of contact while moving around in a kayak

   b. practice proper retrieval should you drop something over the side into the water

   c. both a and b

   d. none of the above

17. Paddlers need to be prepared for

   a. low light conditions

   b. minor medical emergencies

   c. other traffic

   d. all of the above

18. A person standing thigh deep in a 5-mile-per-hour (8 kilometer per hour) current can easily have 100 pounds (45 kilograms) of pressure placed on his legs by the water.

   a. true

   b. false

19. The slowest current is found on the bottom of the river and just next to the surface.

   a. true

   b. false

20. As the river goes around a bend, the faster and deeper current is found on the outside of the bend.

   a. true

   b. false

21. When paddling through rapids, look for downstream Vs and avoid the upstream Vs.

   a. true

   b. false

22. A hole or hydraulic is created by the water filling in the void from the sides behind an exposed rock.

    a. true

    b. false

23. An eddy is created by an obstruction in the water where the water flows over the obstruction and attempts to fill in the void behind the obstruction.

    a. true

    b. false

24. Avoid smiling holes. They are extremely dangerous.

    a. true

    b. false

25. There are three parts to an eddy. There is an upstream portion, a neutral portion where the water is flowing neither upstream nor downstream, and a downstream component where the water moves more slowly downstream than the main current.

    a. true

    b. false

26. Microcurrents are currents found within other currents.

    a. true

    b. false

27. Explain the difference between cold-water shock and hypothermia.

28. List the most typical symptoms of hypothermia in the general order of occurrence.

Chapter 6

1. The purpose of kayak strokes is to make the kayak go where you want it to go.

    a. true

    b. false

2. There are three levels of strokes: basic, compound, and customized strokes.

    a. true

    b. false

3. A compound stroke is defined as adding two or more basic strokes to make a stroke.

    a. true

    b. false

4. The forward, back, and draw strokes are examples of compound strokes.

   a. true

   b. false

5. One indication that a paddler is performing a customized stroke is that she is continuously adjusting the blade angle and the motion of travel of the blade to make the kayak go where she wants it to go.

   a. true

   b. false

6. In a stationary or static stroke, the paddle remains stationary and the force of the water against the paddle moves or turns the kayak.

   a. true

   b. false

7. A dynamic stroke has three phases: catch, propulsion, and recovery.

   a. true

   b. false

8. The J-lean involves leaning the boat and body like a bell buoy.

   a. true

   b. false

9. A stroke applied close to the center line generally propels the kayak forward.

   a. true

   b. false

10. Having knees and thighs against the hull, feet on foot braces, and hips snug in the seat provides more stability in a kayak than simply sitting on the seat.

    a. true

    b. false

11. When the kayak is sitting level in the water front to back, it is said to be in trim.

    a. true

    b. false

12. To keep your kayak upright, keep your shoulders centered over the center line of the boat.

    a. true

    b. false

13. A stationary draw relies on the kayak's moving through the water to turn the boat.

    a. true

    b. false

14. Knowing how to edge the boat, sit up straight, and hold the paddle correctly are all prerequisites to developing a kayaking finesse.
    a. true
    b. false

15. Strokes generally use a paddler's torso muscles for power and arm muscles for positioning.
    a. true
    b. false

16. Holding the paddle at a lifting angle lifts water and does not move the boat efficiently.
    a. true
    b. false

17. When paddling in reverse, flip the paddle face over to use the power face.
    a. true
    b. false

18. Speed, power, and the crossing angle are all important when crossing the current differentials on a river.
    a. true
    b. false

Chapter 7

1. A well-protected launch zone is the best situation for beginners starting an outing.
   a. true
   b. false

2. Launching a sea kayak in swells is very easy.
   a. true
   b. false

3. Waves are chaotic with no pattern. Each paddler must fend for herself.
   a. true
   b. false

4. A wave break is caused when water depth becomes deeper than the height of the wave.
   a. true
   b. false

5. Nautical charts are a must for long day trips and open water crossings.
   a. true
   b. false

6. Strong currents in channel crossings require special strategies to maintain the bearing to your destination.
   a. true
   b. false

7. A wind coming from any direction except head-on or directly behind the sea kayaker tends to weathervane the boat, sweeping it sideways toward the destination.
   a. true
   b. false

8. Sea kayaking is not as risky as whitewater kayaking.
   a. true
   b. false

9. Assuming powerboaters cannot see you is a good safety attitude.
   a. true
   b. false

10. Carrying a two-way radio or cellular phone when paddling open waters can simplify a rescue situation.
    a. true
    b. false

11. Which type of signals are not suitable for nighttime use?
    a. smoke flares
    b. parachute flares
    c. strobe lights
    d. handheld or aerial flares

12. Sea kayakers should always carry signaling devices.
    a. true
    b. false

13. Fetch is the distance wind travels unrestricted across the water.
    a. true
    b. false

14. It is good safety to paddle in the middle of channels with powerboats to ensure they see you.
    a. true
    b. false

15. When crossing a channel, go straight across or at a right angle to the channel.
    a. true
    b. false

16. Navigational channels are marked with green (triangular-shaped) and red (square shaped) markers.

    a. true

    b. false

17. Many sea kayaking skills require experience to apply. Reading about them is only the first step in the learning process.

    a. true

    b. false

Chapter 8

1. There are few skills learned on flatwater that apply to whitewater.

    a. true

    b. false

2. Foot entrapment can be avoided by not standing in current greater than knee deep.

    a. true

    b. false

3. Strainers may be formed by trees lying across the current and should be avoided.

    a. true

    b. false

4. Undercut rocks are easy to spot in a river.

    a. true

    b. false

5. Killer hydraulics may form behind a human-made dam or a natural ledge.

    a. true

    b. false

6. A boater can be pinned by dropping vertically over a high drop.

    a. true

    b. false

7. To fully prepare for what lies downstream in a river, a paddler should learn to watch the water directly under the boat's bow.

    a. true

    b. false

8. The most important component of a ferry is the lean downstream.

    a. true

    b. false

9. In a forward ferry, the paddler faces upstream.
   a. true
   b. false

10. An eddy turn is a rodeo move not needed by the typical river paddler.
    a. true
    b. false

11. A peelout is a natural move not needing a special approach.
    a. true
    b. false

12. Current speed is easy to estimate.
    a. true
    b. false

13. Wind has the biggest impact on trip quality if there are open expanses or canyons with strong wind that can impede progress.
    a. true
    b. false

Chapter 9

1. Each paddler has an opportunity and a responsibility to care for the water resource.
   a. true
   b. false

2. Only healthy people should paddle.
   a. true
   b. false

3. Kayaking is an activity that is available only to the wealthy.
   a. true
   b. false

4. Paddlers have unrestricted access to any of the nation's waterways.
   a. true
   b. false

5. Paddlers should be concerned about all activities that have an impact on the resource, including personal toilet activity.
   a. true
   b. false

6. Urinating directly in the water may be advisable on certain desert water-ways or at sea.

   a. true

   b. false

7. You should plan to dispose of any foodstuff in the same location as human waste to consolidate the spread of waste.

   a. true

   b. false

8. To view wildlife, allow your craft to drift into any animals or birds you find swimming or wading.

   a. true

   b. false

9. To minimize impacts to the shore when launching, portaging, scouting, or taking out, do not drag boats on the ground, and avoid stepping on vegetation.

   a. true

   b. false

10. Paddlers need to know the rules of navigation for use when paddling on multiple-use waterways.

    a. true

    b. false

11. The three strategic tenets of the American Canoe Association are education, stewardship, and recreation.

    a. true

    b. false

12. Paddling clubs are a great way to continue paddling and gain extensive experience.

    a. true

    b. false

Answers

Chapter 1: 1. false; 2. false; 3. true; 4. true; 5. false; 6. false; 7. true; 8. true

Chapter 2: 1. true; 2. false; 3. false; 4. true; 5. true; 6. false; 7. true; 8. false; 9. true; 10. true; 11. c; 12. c; 13. e; 14. b; 15. d; 16. c; 17. d; 18. c; 19. e; 20. e

Chapter 3: 1. false; 2. false; 3. true; 4. true; 5. false; 6. false; 7. true; 8. false; 9. true; 10. false; 11. false; 12. true; 13. true; 14. true; 15. true; 16. true; 17. false; 18. false; 19. true

Chapter 4: 1. true; 2. false; 3. true; 4. true; 5. true; 6. true; 7. true; 8. true; 9. true; 10. false; 11. true; 12. false; 13. false; 14. false; 15. true; 16. true; 17. false

Chapter 5: 1. true; 2. d; 3. false 4. false; 5. true; 6. outside; 7. eddy; 8. a; 9. true; 10. b; 11. c; 12. d; 13. true; 14. a; 15. true; 16. c; 17. d; 18. true; 19. true; 20. true; 21. true; 22. false; 23. false; 24. false; 25. true; 26. true

27. Cold-water shock is the sudden exposure of the head and chest to cold water. It typically causes an involuntary gasp for air, sudden increases in heart rate and blood pressure, and disorientation and can possibly cause cardiac arrest.

    Hypothermia results when exposure to cold temperatures (air or water) prevents the body from maintaining its normal temperature in the core region (heart, lungs, and the rest of the torso).

28. Shivering, impaired judgment, clumsiness, loss of manual dexterity, slurred speech, inward behavior and withdrawal, cessation of shivering, muscle rigidity, unconsciousness

Chapter 6: 1. true; 2. true; 3. true; 4. false; 5. true; 6. true; 7. true; 8. false; 9. true; 10. true; 11. true; 12. true; 13. true; 14. true; 15. true; 16. true; 17. false; 18. true

Chapter 7: 1. true; 2. false; 3. false; 4. false; 5. true; 6. true; 7. true; 8. false; 9. true; 10. true; 11. a; 12. true; 13. true; 14. false; 15. true; 16. false; 17. true

Chapter 8: 1. false; 2. true; 3. true; 4. false; 5. true; 6. true; 7. false; 8. false; 9. true; 10. false; 11. false; 12. false; 13. true

Chapter 9: 1. true; 2. false; 3. false; 4. false; 5. true; 6. true; 7. false; 8. false; 9. true; 10. true; 11. true; 12. true

Photo Credits

About the Editors

Pamela S. Dillon, American Canoe Association executive director from 2002 to 2007, has been an avid paddler since the early 1970s. She has served as an ACA instructor trainer (IT) in canoe and kayak.

Appointed as chief of the Ohio Department of Natural Resources Division of Watercraft in 2007, Pamela returned to her roots, where she began as a state watercraft officer in 1977. With ODNR she assisted in the development of the Ohio River Rescue Training program, the first state-sponsored training program of its kind in the United States. Pamela served as chair of the National Safe Boating Council (NSBC) from 1991 to 1993. In 2005, she was appointed to the National Boating Safety Advisory Council (NBSAC) and was reappointed for a second term through 2009. She was named to the National Boating Safety Hall of Fame in 2006.

For her work, Pamela has received recognition from the U.S. Coast Guard, National Association of State Boating Law Administrators, National Safe Boating Council, National Water Safety Congress, Professional Paddlesports Association, and United States Power Squadrons. She has also received numerous federal, state, and local awards.

Jeremy Oyen is the American Canoe Association director of safety education and instruction. He has worked in the paddlesports and outdoor education field for over 20 years. He has served as a wilderness canoe guide, whitewater canoe and kayak instructor, manager of a specialty outdoor retail shop, paddlesports buyer, owner of Lake Erie's first sea kayak guide company, and manager of Cleveland Metroparks' nationally recognized Institute of the Great Outdoors, where he received the International Boating and Water Safety Summit's National Boating Education and Advancement Award in 2005. He holds a secondary education teaching license in the State of Ohio and ACA certifications as an instructor trainer educator in coastal kayaking, an instructor trainer in adaptive paddling, and an instructor of river canoeing (solo and tandem) and river kayaking.

About the Contributors

Kent Ford's unique background includes 30 years of teaching paddling, international whitewater slalom racing, winning world titles, coaching for the U.S. kayak team, and working as an announcer at the last five Olympic Games. Now Kent focuses on teaching recreational boating to a worldwide audience. His 20 videos and books have influenced the education of half a million paddlers and have made him one of the most recognized paddlers in whitewater sport worldwide. Best of all, Kent's teaching style is enthusiastic, supportive, and open-minded. As an ACA instructor trainer, Kent has led programs at most major U.S. paddle schools as well as in Switzerland, Canada, and Japan. A veteran of over 340 rivers in 28 countries, Kent has been a member of expeditions to the Soviet Union, Costa Rica, Turkey, and Mexico.

Kent holds a BS in mechanical engineering from Carnegie-Mellon University and resides in Durango, Colorado. A volunteer member of the City of Durango's water commission, Kent advocates for sustainable water policy. His pro bono video productions on threats to the Dolores and Animas Rivers helped stimulate advocacy and protection on their behalf. Other recent projects include organizing the Whitewater Symposium, an industry roundtable supporting the health of paddlesports.

Mike Aronoff is an instructor trainer of ACA open-water coastal kayak, river kayak, and whitewater canoe. He is also a swiftwater rescue instructor as well as a British Canoe Union coach. In 2006 he was vice chair of the ACA Safety Education and Instruction Committee and in 2006-2007 was chair of the Coastal Kayak Committee. Currently he chairs the ACA Introduction to Paddling Committee and is active on the River Kayak and Coastal Kayak Committees.

Mike owns Canoe, Kayak and Paddle Co. LLC, the first ACA professional school. His company provides instruction and trip leading for kayak and canoe at all levels. The company also donates 10 percent of all profits to environmental charities. Mike is an adjunct professor of kayaking at George Mason University and also teaches kayaking at the University of Maryland, Loyola College in Baltimore, and the College of the Albemarle in North Carolina.

Wyatt Boughter, a former professional in the paddlesports industry, resides with his wife and black Lab in Phoenixville, PA where he supports his paddling habits as a graphic designer. Wyatt is proud to be an ACA lifetime member and instructor of both canoe and kayak. When not on the water he can be found behind the lens of his camera or happily attached to his black lab, Stanza.

Virgil Chambers has been the executive director of the National Safe Boating Council since 1996. He is retired from the State of Pennsylvania, where he was the chief of the Boating Safety and Education Division for the Pennsylvania Fish and Boat Commission from 1978 to 1996. He developed and started the Pennsylvania Public School Boating and Water Safety program. He is the founder of the National Association for Search and Rescue (NASAR) water rescue training program and was the director of this national program from 1987 to 1997. He received the National Association of State Boating Law Administrators boating safety education award in 1994 and has been recognized with many other awards by national and international organizations for his work in boating and water safety education. He is in the Pennsylvania Swimming Hall of Fame at Pennsylvania State University. He was chair of the Ohio-Penn Division of the American Canoe Association from 1996 to 2002. Virgil is certified as a lifeguard instructor, water safety instructor, canoeing and kayaking instructor, and boating safety instructor with the American Red Cross, American Canoe Association, and National Safe Boating Council, respectively.

Dr. Robert Kauffman is a professor and chair of recreation and park management at Frostburg State University. As part of his academic responsibilities, he coordinates the FSU component of a collaborative program with Garrett Community College in adventure sports. Recently, he served on the board of directors of the American Canoe Association, where he served as secretary for the association. In addition, he served on the ACA's council between 1980 and 1989 and obtained the Coast Guard grants for the hypothermia film *Cold, Wet and Alive* and the river rescue film *Heads Up*.

Under a Coast Guard grant, he authored a boating safety text for use in state boating safety programs, titled *Boating Fundamentals: A Manual for Safe Boating*. His paddlesport-oriented articles have appeared in *Park and Recreation* magazine,